Mathematics Assessment

A PRACTICAL

Handbook

FOR GRADES 6–8

CLASSROOM ASSESSMENT
FOR SCHOOL MATHEMATICS

Edited by

William S. Bush

Steve Leinwand

Grades 6–8 Writing Team

Pam Beck

Lise Dworkin

Steve Leinwand

Jimmy Rios

Ann Rainey

Lynn Raith

Mathematics Assessment

A PRACTICAL

Handbook

FOR GRADES 6–8

NCTM

NATIONAL COUNCIL OF
TEACHERS OF MATHEMATICS

Copyright © 2000 by
THE NATIONAL COUNCIL OF TEACHERS OF MATHEMATICS, INC.
1906 Association Drive, Reston, VA 20191-1502
(703) 620-9840; (800) 235-7566; www.nctm.org

Fourth printing 2005

Library of Congress Cataloging-in-Publication Data

Mathematics assessment : a practical handbook for grades 6–8 / edited by William
S. Bush, Steve Leinwand ; grades 6–8 writing team Pam Beck ... [et al.].
      p. cm. — (Classroom assessment for school mathematics K—12)
Includes bibliographical references and index.
ISBN 0-87353-481-6
      1. Mathematics–Study and teaching (Middle school)—United States
—Evaluation. I. Bush, William S. II. Leinwand, Steve. III. Beck, Pam. IV. Series.

QA13 .M153 2000
510'.71'273—dc21

00-028378

The National Council of Teachers of Mathematics is a public voice of mathematics
education, providing vision, leadership, and professional development to support
teachers in ensuring mathematics learning of the highest quality for all students.

Printed in the United States of America

Table of Contents

ACKNOWLEDGMENTS

We wish to thank the educators listed below for their suggestions, examples, and student work. We applaud their willingness to explore new ways to assess their students and, more so, their willingness to share their ideas with us.

Audrey Adams	Donna Foley
Jerry Barrowman	Donna Goldenstein
Sylvia Bednarski	Delia Levine
Mary Benion	Suzanne McGrath
Susan Killebrew	Richard Meyers
Debra Coggin	Paula Ogi
Pam Curtis	Faye Stevens

THE ASSESSMENT ADDENDA TASK FORCE

William S. Bush, *Chair*

Charles Allen

Florence Glanfield

Anja S. Greer

Steve Leinwand

Jean Kerr Stenmark

Dear Reader,

The National Council of Teachers of Mathematics asked our Task Force to create an Addenda Series to support the Assessment Standards for School Mathematics. *This book, one of six books in the series, focuses on classroom assessment in grades 6–8. Three other handbooks for teachers in grades K–2, 3–5, and 9–12 also contain practical examples and ideas from teachers who have been successful with assessment. Two Assessment Cases books present descriptions of real classrooms, students, and teachers in assessment situations. They include reflective questions to encourage discussion about important issues in assessment.*

The Assessment Standards *book tells us that classroom assessment should—*

- *provide a rich variety of mathematical topics and problem situations;*

- *give students opportunities to investigate problems in many ways;*

- *question and listen to students;*

- *look for evidence of learning from many sources;*

- *expect students to use concepts and procedures effectively in solving problems.*

Our collection of examples, reflections, explanations, and tips will help all of us explore the role of assessment in reshaping mathematics teaching and learning. We know that assessment, from simple observations to standardized tests, has always affected what we do in the classroom. We looked for examples that help us do a better job and that allow us to become more clear about what we really want students to learn.

We also know that classrooms and schools are complex environments. Changing assessment practices in nonsupportive environments is challenging at best. We will share the experiences and stories of teachers who have had some success.

We value the role of students in the assessment process—from setting goals to designing and using rubrics to sharing results with others. Students have specific rights while being assessed. We have adapted a list of students' rights developed by Grant Wiggins (1996) and included them on the next page. Please read them and think about how they affect classroom assessment.

Many people contributed to this effort. We sought the advice of teachers who have been successful with classroom assessment. We looked for the kinds of assessment that happen in classrooms, carried out by teachers and the students themselves. We found examples of assessment that accurately reflect what teachers believe important and what students are studying and learning. These examples are the most important part of the books.

This book, A Practical Handbook for Grades 6–8, is divided into three sections. The first, Practical Suggestions and Examples, includes four chapters that offer a wealth of advice about getting ready to change assessment practices, selecting and developing assessment tools, implementing an assessment system, and using the results of assessment. The second section includes twenty samples of assessment tasks developed by groups of teachers. We have printed these tasks in a form to be copied. So, feel free to duplicate them as needed. The last section includes a bibliography of reflective readings about assessment. Finally, we have provided an index at the end to help you locate topics of greatest interest to you.

We hope you will find many uses for this series. Enjoy!

Every student has a right to—

■ do interesting work that is useful, challenging, intriguing, or provocative;

■ work collaboratively with the teacher to make learning meaningful;

■ know the well-defined and clearly stated criteria for assessment or grading;

■ be judged according to established criteria rather than according to her or his rank among competitors;

■ get genuine and frequent feedback, both for right now and for long-term progress toward the exit level;

■ take part in grading or scoring that will give chances to improve performance, with assessment being recursive and continual;

■ have plenty of opportunity to do work of which he or she can be proud, with revisions, self-assessment, and self-correction;

■ be able to show, often and in many ways, how well she or he is doing, especially to demonstrate strengths;

■ use during assessment whatever resources (calculators, rulers, reference books, manipulatives, etc.) were available during learning.

*Mathematics
Assessment:
A Practical
Handbook for
Grades 6–8*

Introduction

This is a book about assessment in the middle school mathematics classroom. We hope that the information contained in this book will provide you with practical tools and provocative suggestions for classroom assessment. When we use the word "assessment," we refer to attempts to answer the following questions:

- How can I communicate my expectations about my students' mathematical understanding and the quality of their work?

- What do I think my students understand at this point in time? What do they think they understand?

- Does the question, task, or activity that I choose raise the mathematical issues I hope it will raise for my students? Does it provide an opportunity for them to show me what they know?

- What question, task, or activity should I pose next?

- How can I communicate to my students and others what I think they understand?

We see classroom assessment as the centerpiece of the work teachers do. We know that teachers assess their students continually, both informally (by listening, observing, and interacting with students in class) and formally (through homework, quizzes, tests, and projects).

The ideas in this book come from our own classroom experience and from the experience of colleagues from around the country. We have been guided in our work, and in writing this book, by the vision of mathematics curriculum and instruction framed in a series of influential documents, *Curriculum and Evaluation Standards for School Mathematics* (National Council of Teachers of Mathematics [NCTM] 1989), *Professional Standards for Teaching Mathematics* (NCTM 1991), *Measuring What Counts; A Conceptual Guide for Mathematics Assessment* (Mathematical Sciences Education Board [MSEB] 1993), and in particular by these standards taken from *Assessment Standards for School Mathematics* (NCTM 1995):

Standard 1: Assessment should enhance mathematics learning.

Standard 2: Assessment should promote equity.

Standard 3: Assessment should be an open process.

Standard 4: Assessment should promote valid inferences about mathematics learning.

Standard 5: Assessment should be a coherent process.

We have organized our presentation into four chapters. In the first, we set the stage by making the case for considering new ways to assess students.

The second chapter focuses on assessment tasks; specifically how to find, modify, and create them. In the third chapter, we offer ways to plan and conduct a coherent classroom assessment program. We conclude this part of the book with a discussion of scoring, grading, reporting, and using the assessment data we collect.

Each chapter contains these features:

- **Teacher-to-Teacher** and **Student-to-Teacher** letters

- Definitions of common terms (e.g., open-ended task, analytic rubric)

- **Tips from Teachers**

- Examples of tasks, student work, rubrics, and strategies for scoring and grading

- Responses to frequently-asked questions

- References to primary sources

- References to the accompanying case books

We believe that all students are capable of developing mathematical power. We also believe that how we assess students affects this development in fundamental ways. We hope this handbook, and its companion case book, provide you with the practical suggestions that you need. We also hope they provoke you to think about assessment in new ways, and that they stimulate discussion among you, your students, and your colleagues about this crucial aspect of the work of teachers.

—The 6-8 Writing Team

# Chapter 1

Getting Ready to Shift Assessment Practices: How Do I Get Started?

Teacher-to-Teacher

How well am I doing? That's what I really need to know. I have been teaching eighth-grade math for a few years now. I still have so many questions about what I am doing. Are my students ready for the material I am about to teach? Do my instructional strategies work? Do my students understand the mathematics I have taught? Should I reteach a particular concept or skill? Have my students retained the material I taught and used it in new situations? Can my students apply what they have learned?

I have been trying to do more problem solving and exploration in my class. I ask my students to explain much more than I used to. I am using more small groups and manipulatives, and the students seem to enjoy them. From using these groups and manipulatives, I have some idea what my students can do. But I don't feel that they are giving me the whole picture. I know I need to try other ways to find out what my students know and can do.

But, I am concerned. Am I ready to begin doing things differently? Why should I bother considering changing what I do? How can I start shifting how I assess my students? How can I make this transition easier?

Getting Started

AM I READY TO BEGIN DOING THINGS DIFFERENTLY?

For many of us, the prime motivation for change is the nagging sense that what we are doing is not working as well as we would like. For example, we find ourselves wondering—

■ whether it is time to try something new to reach our students;

■ whether a correct answer is as important as the thinking used to arrive at that answer;

■ how better to blend daily instruction and assessment;

■ whether grades of A or C+ really communicate what students really know and can do;

■ why students who ask great questions do poorly on weekly tests.

Similarly, many of us have come to realize that—

■ most good mathematics problems have more than one correct answer and several appropriate solution paths;

■ tests and quizzes are only one way to assess mathematical understanding;

■ available technology challenges what we value mathematically and how we teach and assess mathematics;

■ diverse student styles, interests, and preferences require diverse forms of assessment.

If these are among the things that you believe or that you have thought about, then it is likely you are either ready to begin doing things a little differently in your classroom or that you have already started making changes.

Chapter Overview

The NCTM *Assessment Standards for School Mathematics* describes a set of shifts necessary to change assessment practices. Review these shifts in **figure 1.1** below.

WHY SHOULD I BOTHER CONSIDERING CHANGING WHAT I DO?

Compare the left- and right-hand columns in the "Major Shifts in Assessment Practice" at the bottom of the page. Which is harder—the left column or the right column? When we were students, assessment seemed pretty straightforward: we learned the skills and concepts of a new topic for two or so weeks; we completed assignments that focused on one or two new skills; we took a 45-minute test; and we received a grade based on the average of several tests. With only slight exaggeration, this sequence describes how we might have been assessed in middle school mathematics classes.

FIG. 1.1

MAJOR SHIFTS IN ASSESSMENT PRACTICE (from National Council of Teachers of Mathematics [NCTM] 1995, p. 83)

TOWARD	AWAY FROM
Assessing students' full mathematical power	Assessing only students' knowledge of specific facts and isolated skills
Comparing students' performance with established criteria	Comparing students' performance with that of other students
Giving support to teachers and credence to their informed judgement	Designing teacher-proof assessment systems
Making the assessment process public, participatory, and dynamic	Making the assessment process secret, exclusive, and fixed
Giving students multiple opportunities to demonstrate their full mathematical power	Restricting students to a single way of demonstrating their mathematical knowledge
Developing a shared vision of what to assess and how to do it	Developing assessment by oneself
Using assessment results to ensure that all students have the opportunity to achieve their potential	Using assessment to filter and select students out of the opportunities to learn mathematics
Aligning assessment with curriculum and instruction	Treating assessment as independent of curriculum or instruction
Basing inferences on multiple sources of evidence	Basing inferences on restricted or single sources of evidence
Viewing students as active participants in the assessment process	Viewing students as the objects of assessment
Regarding assessment as continual and recursive	Regarding assessment as sporadic and conclusive
Holding all concerned with mathematics learning accountable for assessment results	Holding only a few accountable for assessment results

Getting Started

READ ABOUT...

■ *Read about two middle school teachers' struggle with starting new assessment approaches in "Does It Measurement Up?" and "Tessellation Presentation" in* Mathematics Assessment: Cases and Discussion Questions for Grades 6–12 *(Bush 1999).*

■ *Read more about getting started with assessment in "Planning for Classroom Portfolio Assessment" by Diana Lambdin and Vicki Walker (1996) and in "Journal Writing: An Insight into Students' Understanding" by Karen Norwood and Glenda Carter (1994).*

Listed in **figure** 1.2 below are a set of statements taken from different sources. They describe reasons some people believe that assessment practices should change.

FIG. 1.2

REASONS ASSESSMENT NEEDS TO CHANGE

Getting Started

HOW CAN I BEGIN CHANGING THE WAY I ASSESS MY STUDENTS?

Ask students to write about or explain how they created their work. You are well on your way when you use—

- essay-type questions or assignments;
- questions asking students to show conclusions or to make inferences;
- questions that allow students to present or argue their point of view;
- students' presentations of projects or homework assignments.

HOW CAN I MAKE THIS TRANSITION EASIER?

Relax, take some risks, and don't worry if things get a little messy. The following are what some teachers keep in mind as they assess their students.

Secrets to Getting Off to a Good Start

— *Start Small* —

— *Go Slow* —

— *Maintain Momentum* —

— *Stay Comfortable* —

TIPS FROM TEACHERS

- *Don't expect that every task or assignment is going to be a worthwhile contribution.*

- *Don't score every piece of student work.*

- *Don't panic when you encounter students' work that you don't understand. Explore further.*

- *Make sure scoring schemes or rubrics are easy to use and clear to students and parents.*

- *Accept the fact that there will never be enough time.*

- *Use short writing assignments that ask students to reflect on some mathematical topic or on their ideas about what happened in class.*

- *Ask "Why?" and "How do you know?" or "Explain what you did" as often as possible.*

- *Pick a topic or issue to monitor during one or two class meetings and try to document what is found out about the issue.*

- *Share as much students' work with the class as possible.*

- *Create or borrow a simple rubric (Wow, Okay, Hmmm, Yucky) to score student work.*

- *Gather students' work in mini-portfolios or in smaller collections over a short period of time.*

- *Try one new idea at a time.*

Aligning Instruction and Assessment

TIPS FROM TEACHERS

■ *Encourage the mathematics teachers to meet regularly to discuss goals.*

■ *Develop assessments as you plan units so that assessment aligns with unit goals.*

■ *Sort and classify assessments according to the district's instructional goals as you gather them.*

■ *Seek parent input about goals during parent conferences.*

■ *Review students' work carefully before planning the next unit.*

■ *Gather information about students' learning and performance as you teach.*

■ *Use assessment results to plan future lessons.*

READ ABOUT...

■ *Read more about aligning instruction and assessment in "Integrating Assessment and Instruction" by Donald Chambers (1993) and "Linking Instruction and Assessment in the Mathematics Classroom" by Kay Sammons, Beth Kobett, Joan Heiss, and Francis Fennell (1992).*

■ *Video units entitled "Fraction Tracks" and "Building Rods" from the WGBH Assessment Library (1998) present excellent examples of how middle school mathematics teachers have aligned assessment and instruction in their classes.*

Perhaps the most important reason for shifting assessment practices is to make sure our curriculum goals, instructional methods, and assessment practices align. The NCTM *Curriculum and Evaluation Standards for School Mathematics* (1989, p.193) summarizes the issue clearly:

> The assessment of students' mathematics learning should enable educators to draw conclusions about their instructional needs, their progress in achieving the goals of the curriculum, and the effectiveness of a mathematics program. The degree to which meaningful inferences can be drawn from such an assessment depends on the degree to which the assessment methods and tasks are aligned or are in agreement with the curriculum. Little information is produced about students' mastery of curricular topics when the assessment methods and tasks do not reflect curricular goals, objectives, and content; the instructional emphasis of the mathematics program; or how the material is taught.

Considerable thought and effort are required to align state, provincial, or district instructional goals with textbook curriculum goals and with our assessment practices.

HOW DO I ALIGN INSTRUCTION AND ASSESSMENT?

Having a picture of what aligned assessment and instruction look like in our classroom can help. Classroom videos of teachers in action and stories written by teachers provide excellent examples of how instruction and assessment might be aligned. Below are some excellent resources:

■ The Assessment Library from the WGBH Educational Foundation

■ PBS MATHLINE videotapes

■ Teachers stories compiled by Marilyn Burns and Cathy McLaughlin in *A Collection of Math Lessons from Grades 6 through 8* (Burns and McLaughlin 1990)

SOMETHING TO THINK ABOUT

Ask your colleagues what it means to them to align assessment and instruction. Ask them if blending instruction and assessment is an important goal. Ask them how they know whether or not they are doing it.

Making Choices

WHAT ASSESSMENT CHOICES DO I HAVE?

Many choices will arise as we try new approaches to assessment. The further we go on the assessment journey, the more choices we have. In **figure 1.3** are just some of the choices that will arise as you change your assessment practices.

Some excellent sources to for your assessment library include *Mathematics Assessment: Myths, Models, Good Questions, and Practical Suggestions*, edited by Jean Stenmark (1991); *Assessment Alternatives in Mathematics* by David Clarke (1988); *Assessment in the Mathematics Classroom*, 1993 Yearbook of the National Council of Teachers of Mathematics, edited by Norman Webb (1993); and *Emphasis on Assessment*: *Readings from NCTM's School-Based Journals*, edited by Diana Lambdin, Paul Kehle, and Ronald Preston (1996).

FIG. 1.3

TYPES OF ASSESSMENT CHOICES AND SAMPLE QUESTIONS

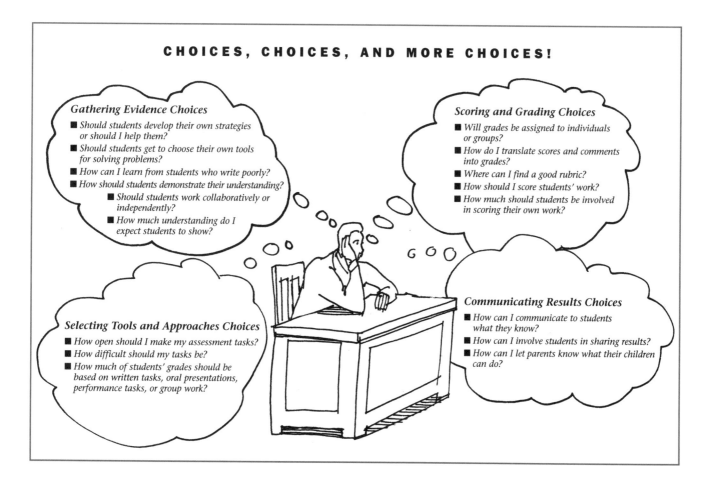

CHOICES, CHOICES, AND MORE CHOICES!

Gathering Evidence Choices
- Should students develop their own strategies or should I help them?
- Should students get to choose their own tools for solving problems?
- How can I learn from students who write poorly?
- How should students demonstrate their understanding?
  - Should students work collaboratively or independently?
  - How much understanding do I expect students to show?

Scoring and Grading Choices
- Will grades be assigned to individuals or groups?
- How do I translate scores and comments into grades?
- Where can I find a good rubric?
- How should I score students' work?
- How much should students be involved in scoring their own work?

Selecting Tools and Approaches Choices
- How open should I make my assessment tasks?
- How difficult should my tasks be?
- How much of students' grades should be based on written tasks, oral presentations, performance tasks, or group work?

Communicating Results Choices
- How can I communicate to students what they know?
- How can I involve students in sharing results?
- How can I let parents know what their children can do?

Chapter 2

Selecting and Developing Tools for Assessment: How Do I Find Out What My Students Know and Can Do?

Teacher-to-Teacher

Okay, I am ready to get started. I'm ready to find out what my students really know and can do mathematically. I think my sixth graders are ready, too. But what do I do now? I have so many different things I want to know about my students. How well do they understand mathematics? Can they explain mathematical ideas? Can they do basic mathematics, especially computation? Can they solve difficult problems? How well do they think and reason? Can they apply mathematics to everyday situations? Can they handle large projects? I really don't have the resources to get started. I have all my old tests and quizzes, but I am sure they cannot do the job. Where can I go to find the tasks and strategies to help me answer these questions? Will I have to create my own tasks? How can I get my students more involved in their own assessment?

Assessing Conceptual Understanding

Conceptual understanding is an important goal for mathematics instruction. In order for students to develop mathematics power, they must have a deep understanding of mathematics concepts and their relationships.

WHAT ARE MATHEMATICS CONCEPTS?

Concepts are the building blocks of mathematics. They are the foundation on which mathematical understanding is based. We can think of them as the "nouns" of mathematics because they are always objects. One way to think about mathematics concepts is to consider them as a set of objects with a name tag. The picture in **figure 2.1** represents the concept of rational number.

FIG. 2.1

THE CONCEPT OF RATIONAL NUMBER

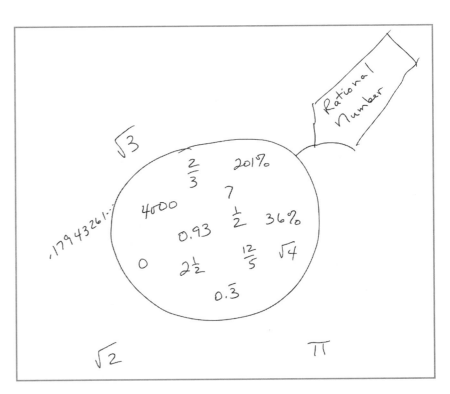

The middle school mathematics curriculum contains many concepts. The following list includes a few of the more important ones:

Important Mathematical Concepts

Rational numbers	Polyhedrons
Integers	Polygons
Fractions	Circles
Percent	Functions
Ratios	Graphs
Proportions	Mean
Exponents	Median
Probability	Mode
Randomness	Volume
Sample Space	Area
Perimeter	Circumference

HOW DO I ASSESS CONCEPTUAL UNDERSTANDING?

To assess students' understanding of mathematics concepts, we might ask them to—

- describe concepts in their own words;

- identify or give examples and nonexamples of concepts;

- use concepts correctly in a variety of situations.

Tasks designed to assess understanding can vary—from focusing narrowly on the concept (as in the previous example) to focusing on the way in which concepts are used. Below is a description of such tasks.

Assessment tasks that focus primarily on mathematical concepts give students a chance to apply a concept in a new situation, to reformulate it, and to express it in their own terms. These tasks probe the understanding of an idea. They are usually—

- nonroutine;

- short;

- based upon reconstruction, rather than memorization;

- cast in a context;

- focused on representation and explanation of the solution.

Chapter Overview

In this chapter you will learn about—

- assessing conceptual understanding, skills, problem solving, attitudes, and beliefs;

- using and selecting different assessment tools—
  - quizzes and tests
  - pieces of work done outside class
  - multiday assignments
  - teacher notes and checklists
  - students' writing and inventories
  - collections of work

- creating your own assessment tasks;

- expanding assessment tasks.

Assessing Conceptual Understanding

WHAT ARE SOME EXAMPLES?

The samples of students' work in **figures 2.2** and **2.3** illustrate how we might assess the concepts of ratios and sample space with sixth-grade students.

Note how the task in **figure 2.2** reveals problems with this student's understanding of ratios. Why did this student respond this way? How can a teacher help the student develop an understanding of ratio?

FIG. 2.2

STUDENT WORK—RATIOS

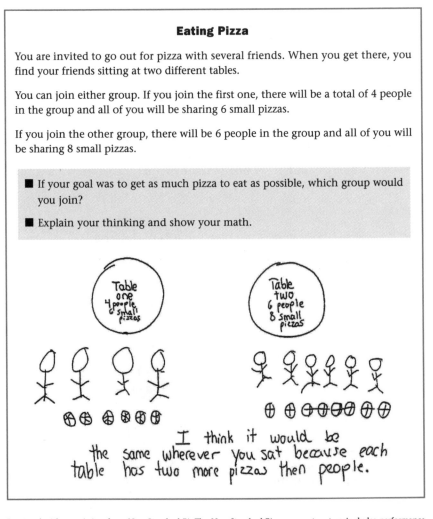

Eating Pizza

You are invited to go out for pizza with several friends. When you get there, you find your friends sitting at two different tables.

You can join either group. If you join the first one, there will be a total of 4 people in the group and all of you will be sharing 6 small pizzas.

If you join the other group, there will be 6 people in the group and all of you will be sharing 8 small pizzas.

- If your goal was to get as much pizza to eat as possible, which group would you join?

- Explain your thinking and show your math.

Reprinted with permission from New Standards™. The New Standards™ assessment system includes performance standards with performance descriptions, student work samples and commentaries, on-demand examinations, and a portfolio system. For more information contact the National Center on Education and the Economy, 202-783-3668 or www.ncee.org.

Assessing Conceptual Understanding

The task in **figure 2.3** focuses on the concept of sample space at grade 8. The challenge for students in this task is to use the concept of "sample space" in a nonroutine situation. Students are not likely to succeed without understanding what sample spaces are.

From the evidence, does the student understand the concept of sample space? How do you know?

FIG. 2.3

STUDENT WORK—FIND SAMPLE SPACE

Ana and May will play a spinner game. These are the rules:

- ■ When it is a player's turn, she spins both spinners.

- ■ Then she adds the two numbers that the arrows point to.

- ■ If the sum is odd (1, 3, 5, 7...), Ana wins, even if it was not her turn.

- ■ If the sum is even (0, 2, 4, 6 ...), May wins, even if it was not her turn.

May tries a test spin first. Here is what she spins.

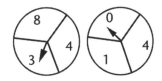

The sum from this spin is 3, because 3 + 0 = 3. Ana wins.

Ana says, "I like this game. I have a better chance to win it than you do."

May says, "No, I have a better chance to win it than you do."

Decide which girl is right.   May is right (even #'s)

Use mathematics to show how you know who has a better chance to win.

M	A
0+8 =8	0+3=3
0+4 =4	4+3=7
4+8 =12	1+8 =9
4+4 =8	1+4=5
1+3 =4	3+0=3
3+1 =4	3+4=7
8+0=8	8+1 =9
8+4=12	4+1=5
4+0=4	
4+4=8	

Reprinted with permission from New Standards™. The New Standards™ assessment system includes performance standards with performance descriptions, student work samples and commentaries, on-demand examinations, and a portfolio system. For more information contact the National Center on Education and the Economy, 202-783-3668 or www.ncee.org.

Assessing Conceptual Understanding

READ ABOUT...

■ *Read about a middle school teacher's struggle with trying to assess her students' understanding of area and perimeter concepts in "Where Did That Question Come From?" in* Mathematics Assessment: Cases and Discussion Questions for Grades 6–12 *(Bush 2000).*

■ *Read more about about assessing concepts in "Promoting Mathematics Connections with Concept Mapping" by Bobbye Bartels (1995), in "Concept Learning in Geometry" by David Fuys and Amy Liebov (1997), and in "Using Concept Diagrams to Promote Understanding in Geometry" by Jean Shaw, Conn Thomas, Ann Hoffman, and Janis Bulgren (1995).*

HOW DO I ASSESS RELATIONSHIPS AMONG CONCEPTS?

Concepts rarely appear in isolation. Mathematics is built on relationships and connections. Therefore, it is important that our students develop an understanding of the relationships among important concepts.

The student's work in **figure 2.4** shows a series of tasks that assesses understanding of the relationships between area and perimeter. Does this student understand how area and perimeter are related? What evidence is provided?

FIG. 2.4

STUDENT WORK—AREA AND PERIMETER

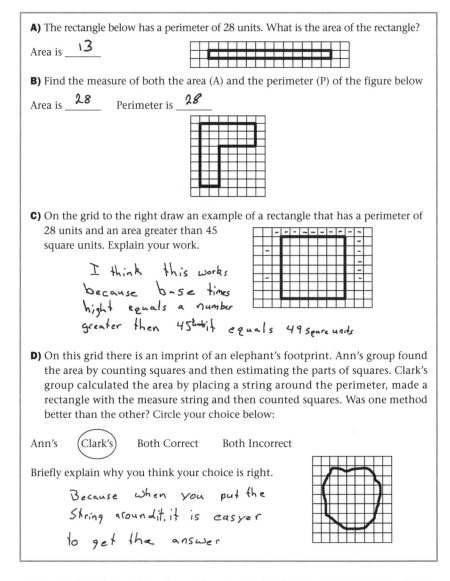

A) The rectangle below has a perimeter of 28 units. What is the area of the rectangle?

Area is ___13___

B) Find the measure of both the area (A) and the perimeter (P) of the figure below

Area is ___28___   Perimeter is ___28___

C) On the grid to the right draw an example of a rectangle that has a perimeter of 28 units and an area greater than 45 square units. Explain your work.

I think this works because base times hight equals a number greater then 45 but if equals 49 square units

D) On this grid there is an imprint of an elephant's footprint. Ann's group found the area by counting squares and then estimating the parts of squares. Clark's group calculated the area by placing a string around the perimeter, made a rectangle with the measure string and then counted squares. Was one method better than the other? Circle your choice below:

Ann's   (Clark's)   Both Correct   Both Incorrect

Briefly explain why you think your choice is right.

Because when you put the String around it, it is easyer to get the answer

This task was adapted from a task in Wilson, Linda Dager, and Sylvia Chavarria, "Superitem Tests as a Classroom Assessment Tool." In *Assessment in the Mathematics Classroom*, 1993 Yearbook of the National Council of Teachers of Mathematics, edited by Norman Webb, pp. 135–42. Reston, Va.: National Council of Teachers of Mathematics, 1993.

Assessing Mathematics Skills

WHAT ARE MATHEMATICAL SKILLS?

Skill development is an important part of doing mathematics. To solve problems, students must be able to perform mathematics skills correctly.

If concepts are the *nouns* of mathematics, then skills are the *verbs*. They are the procedures that enable students to perform mathematical tasks. The middle school mathematics curriculum contains many mathematical skills. Listed below are some of the important skills:

Mathematical Skills

- *Compute with rational numbers and integers*
- *Estimate quantities, computation, and measurements*
- *Measure objects with appropriate tools*
- *Graph data*
- *Find probabilities*
- *Solve equations*
- *Use formulas*

HOW DO I ASSESS MATHEMATICAL SKILLS?

To assess proficiency with mathematical skills, we might ask our students to—

- perform the skill accurately and consistently;
- explain how and why the skill works;
- use the skill in a variety of situations.

Assessing skills, like assessing concepts, can focus narrowly on the skill itself or more broadly on how and why the skill is used. Tasks used to assess skills often have the following similar characteristics.

> An assessment task that focuses primarily on mathematical skills gives students a chance to apply a well-practiced and important procedure or algorithm. These tasks are usually—
>
> - routine;
> - short;
> - based on recalling a well-known procedure;
> - cast in a simple context or no context at all;
> - focused on a single correct answer.

Assessing Mathematics Skills

WHAT ARE SOME EXAMPLES?

The student's work in **figure 2.5** shows how we might assess a student's ability to graph coordinates. How would you assess this student's ability to graph coordinate points? What problems does she have? Why is she making the error?

FIG. 2.5

STUDENT WORK—GRAPHING COORDINATE POINTS

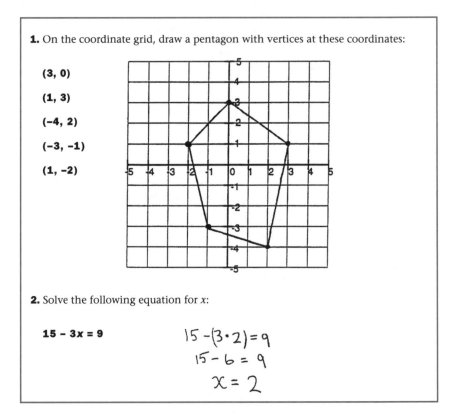

1. On the coordinate grid, draw a pentagon with vertices at these coordinates:

(3, 0)

(1, 3)

(–4, 2)

(–3, –1)

(1, –2)

2. Solve the following equation for x:

15 – 3x = 9

$$15 - (3 \cdot 2) = 9$$
$$15 - 6 = 9$$
$$x = 2$$

Reprinted with permission from New Standards™. The New Standards™ assessment system includes performance standards with performance descriptions, student work samples and commentaries, on-demand examinations, and a portfolio system. For more information contact the National Center on Education and the Economy, 202-783-3668 or www.ncee.org.

Assessing Mathematics Skills

The last question on the previous page should have been difficult to answer on the basis of evidence provided. The task is simply too narrowly focused on the skill. The task in **figure 2.6** is broader and applies the skill of graphing coordinates.

FIG. 2.6

POPCORN SALES

1. The convenience store across the street from Metropolis School has been keeping track of their popcorn sales. The table below shows the total number of bags sold beginning at 6:00 A.M. on a particular day.

   a. Make a coordinate graph of these data. Which variable did you put on the x-axis? Why?

   b. Describe how the number of bags of popcorn sold changed during the day. Explain why these changes may have occurred.

Time	Total bags sold
6:00 A.M.	0
7:00 A.M.	3
8:00 A.M.	15
9:00 A.M.	20
10:00 A.M.	26
11:00 A.M.	30
noon	45
1:00 P.M.	58
2:00 P.M.	58
3:00 P.M.	62
4:00 P.M.	74
5:00 P.M.	83
6:00 P.M.	88
7:00 P.M.	92

From *Connected Mathematics Project: Variables and Patterns*, Student Edition, Gr. 7, by Glenda Lappan, James Fey, William Fitzgerald, Susan Friel, Elizabeth Phillips; Copyright © 1997 by Michigan State University, Glenda Lappan, James Fey, William Fitzgerald, Susan Friel, Elizabeth Phillips. Reprinted with permission of Dale Seymour Publications.

Assessing Mathematics Skills

Figures **2.7** and **2.8** show examples of students' work on this task.

FIG. 2.7

STUDENT WORK—GRAPH OF POPCORN SALES

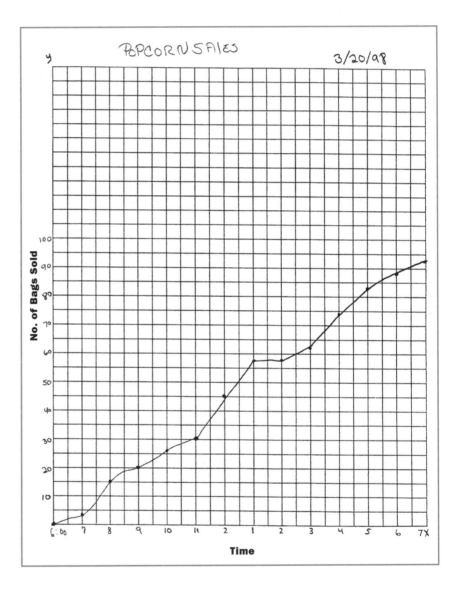

Assessing Mathematics Skills

FIG. 2.8

STUDENT WORK—EXPLANATION OF GRAPH (POPCORN SALES)

PART A   POPCORN SALES

I made Coordinate graph on the class. I had put my line on the x-axis instead of the y-axis. the Number of bags of popcorn are depending on the lines. When I put the Number of bags of pocorn on the x-axis and the line on the y-axis he didn't seem Right cause we couldn't see where the straight, curved lines were.

PART B

The Number of Bags of Popcorn had changed usually Every hour cause at 7-8 you can say kids going in school but didn't have time for Breakfast. 9-10 the students or Some Adults Needed a Snack. 11-1 the Rate went up even more cause It was lunch time and Some People want a light Snack cause after lunch if they are also they will be Ready to take a Nap from 2-7 People Will want a light Snack so they will buy popcorn. That's how the Rate changes.

READ ABOUT...

■ *For a further reading about assessing skill understanding, read "Just Because They Got It Right Does It Mean They Know It?" by Susan Gay and Margaret Thomas (1993).*

■ *Read about the problems a teacher has in assessing skills in "When the Wrong Way Works" in* Mathematics Assessment: Cases and Discussion Questions for Grades K–5 *(Bush 2001).*

Note that the students completing this application task must be able to graph coordinate points. They must understand what the *x*- and *y*-axes are and what a coordinate graph looks like. In addition, they need to be able to make inferences from graphs. Both tasks are appropriate for assessing the skill of graphing coordinates depending on what kind of evidence we wish to gather.

Assessing Mathematics Skills

ASSESSMENT DECISIONS DEPEND ON INSTRUCTIONAL GOALS

The student's work in **figure 2.9** shows how we might assess the skill of measuring the interior angles of a polygon.

What errors did this student make? What are possible reasons for the errors? How might we broaden this assessment to gather more evidence? Read more about expanding assessment tasks later in this chapter.

Decisions about skill assessment rest with our goals for instruction. Sometimes we want to focus on isolated skills; sometimes we are more interested in using skills in different settings.

FIG. 2.9

STUDENT WORK—MEASURING INTERIOR ANGLES OF POLYGONS

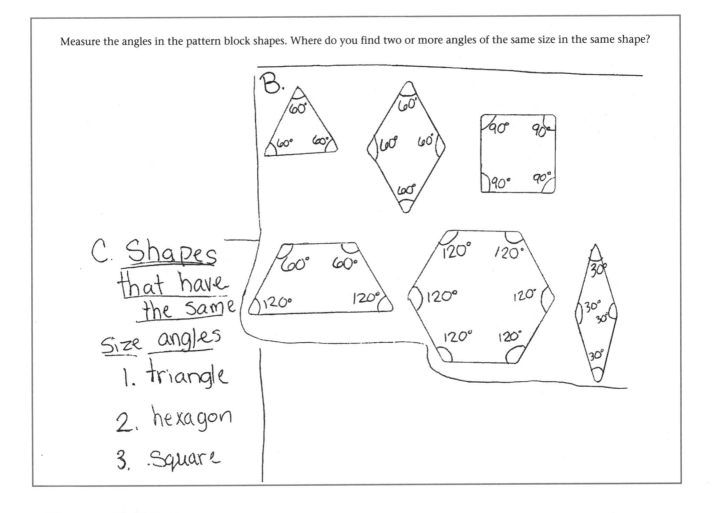

Measure the angles in the pattern block shapes. Where do you find two or more angles of the same size in the same shape?

CHAPTER 2

Assessing Mathematics Problem Solving

According to the NCTM *Standards*, problem solving is the essence of mathematical power. To be successful, students must not only have a clear understanding of mathematics concepts, but they must also be proficient with mathematical skills. And, most important, they must be able to reason mathematically.

WHAT IS MATHEMATICS PROBLEM SOLVING?

Mathematics problem solving has been defined in many ways. We like the definition presented below by Charles and Lester (1982).

A problem is a situation or task for which—

■ *The person confronting the task wants to or needs to find a solution;*

■ *The person has no readily available procedure for finding a solution;*

■ *The person makes an attempt to find a solution;*

■ *A variety of solution routes may be appropriate for solving the problem.*

In summary, the three requirements of problem solving are *desire*, *barrier*, and *effort*. This view of problem solving allows us to include many mathematics tasks as problems—from simple word problems to extended investigations.

One way to think about how mathematics problems are different from one another is through their degrees of "openness." Three definitions are offered in the following box.

CLOSED TASK—Task with one correct answer and one route to arriving at that answer.

OPEN-MIDDLED TASK—Task with one correct answer but many routes to arriving at that answer.

OPEN-ENDED TASK—Task with several correct answers and many routes to arriving at those answers.

Assessing Mathematics Problem Solving

The sets of tasks in **figures 2.10**, **2.11**, and **2.12** focus on different mathematical topics. Each set includes an example of each type of openness.

FIG. 2.10

TASKS ASSESSING PYTHAGOREAN THEOREM

CLOSED TASK:

Myron and Ed want to take a large, square mirror through a doorway. The mirror is 7 feet on each side. The doorway is a rectangle 3 feet wide and $6\frac{1}{2}$ feet tall. Will the mirror fit through the doorway or not? Use the measurements given to calculate your answer and show how you know you are right.

OPEN-MIDDLED TASK:

A company makes metal name plates. The company wants to sell the name plate cemented to a larger wooden square, as shown in the drawing below.

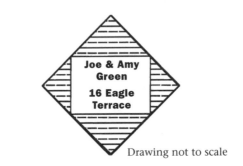

Joe & Amy
Green

16 Eagle
Terrace

Drawing not to scale

The name plates are all rectangles 12 cm by 7 cm. The angles formed where the corners of the nameplate touch the sides of the square are all 45° angles.

Determine the length of each side of the wooden square.

Make the wooden square just large enough that the corners of the metal rectangle touch—but do not hang over—the edge of the square. Show, step by step, how you got your answer.

OPEN-ENDED TASK:

Create a design that tessellates made entirely from triangles. Your design must contain at least two different-shaped triangles; one must be an isosceles right triangle.

Assessing Mathematics Problem Solving

FIG. 2.11

TASKS FOR FRACTIONS

CLOSED TASK:

Mario and Leah went on a bike ride of 52 miles. During the ride Mario asked, "Are we halfway there, yet?" Leah replied, "No, we're about $\frac{3}{8}$ of the way there." How many miles had they gone?

OPEN-MIDDLED TASK:

Nora says both of these figures show $\frac{3}{8}$ of the whole shaded in. Is Nora right or not? Show, step by step, how you decided.

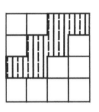

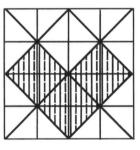

figure a.   figure b.

OPEN-ENDED TASK:

Use a geoboard or grid paper to show different ways to divide a square, 4 units by 4 units, into two regions, where one region is $\frac{3}{8}$ of the whole and the other region is $\frac{5}{8}$ of the whole.

FIG. 2.12

CHECKERBOARD TASKS

CLOSED TASK:

A checkerboard has eight rows of eight 1-unit squares on it. The smallest size square is 1 unit on a side. The largest is 8 units on a side. What are all the other sizes of squares on the checkerboard? How many 1-unit squares does each size square contain?

OPEN-MIDDLED TASK:

How many games of checkers would four people need to play if they wanted to have a tournament in which each person played each of the other people one time? Show how you know you are right.

OPEN-ENDED TASK:

Four students, Ana, Daniel, Julia, and Marc, need a schedule for their checker tournament. In their tournament, each of the four will play each of the other players one time.

■ They want to finish the tournament in one week. They can play from Monday to Friday.

■ They will play only at lunch time. There is enough time during lunch period to play one game of checkers.

■ There are two checker sets, so two games can be going on at once.

■ Marc can't play checkers on the days he is a lunch helper (Monday and Wednesday).

Make a schedule for the tournament. Your schedule should make it easy for everyone to see who plays whom each day.

Assessing Mathematics Problem Solving

READ ABOUT...

■ *Read about a sixth-grade teacher's concerns about the openness of an assessment task in "Open Car Wash" in* Mathematics Assessment: Cases and Discussion Questions for Grades 6–12 *(Bush 2000).*

■ *For more reading about assessing mathematical problem solving, read* How to Evaluate Progress in Problem Solving *by Randall Charles, Frank Lester, and Phares O'Daffer (1987) and "Grading Cooperative Problem Solving" by Diana Kroll, Joanne Masingila, and Sue Mau (1992).*

HOW DO I ASSESS PROBLEM SOLVING?

As illustrated, students must add more information and make more decisions in open-ended tasks. These tasks, however, more often reflect how mathematics is used outside classrooms.

Because problem solving involves understanding, skill, and reasoning, assessment is more complex. The tasks used to assess problem solving are more complex.

An assessment task that focuses primarily on mathematical problem solving gives students a chance to select and use problem-solving strategies. Problem-solving tasks are usually—

■ non-routine;

■ long;

■ predicated on the high-level use of facts, concepts, and skills;

■ cast in a context;

■ focused on the students' abilities to develop and use strategies to solve a problem.

CHAPTER 2

Assessing Mathematics Problem Solving

The task in **figure 2.13** provides an excellent example of problem solving. The main challenges in this task are deciding how to use the information given, figuring the optimum arrangement, and communicating the answer. The concepts needed are not beyond the reach of a sixth grader, but the application of these concepts to the situation makes the task surprisingly challenging for eighth graders. The work shows that this student developed a strategy but was not very successful in implementing it. The student provides an optimum layout but only partially justifies it.

FIG. 2.13

STUDENT WORK—FLEA MARKET

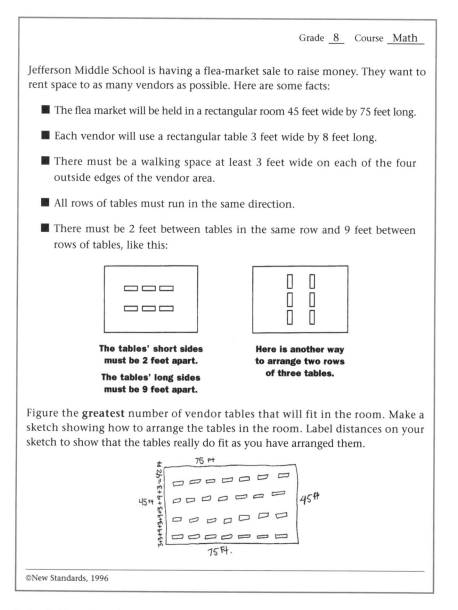

Grade __8__   Course __Math__

Jefferson Middle School is having a flea-market sale to raise money. They want to rent space to as many vendors as possible. Here are some facts:

■ The flea market will be held in a rectangular room 45 feet wide by 75 feet long.

■ Each vendor will use a rectangular table 3 feet wide by 8 feet long.

■ There must be a walking space at least 3 feet wide on each of the four outside edges of the vendor area.

■ All rows of tables must run in the same direction.

■ There must be 2 feet between tables in the same row and 9 feet between rows of tables, like this:

The tables' short sides must be 2 feet apart.

The tables' long sides must be 9 feet apart.

Here is another way to arrange two rows of three tables.

Figure the **greatest** number of vendor tables that will fit in the room. Make a sketch showing how to arrange the tables in the room. Label distances on your sketch to show that the tables really do fit as you have arranged them.

©New Standards, 1996

Assessing Attitudes and Beliefs

Students' attitudes toward mathematics and beliefs about mathematics often affect their mathematics performance. In fact, the NCTM *Standards* includes beliefs and attitudes as two of five goals for instruction: learning to value mathematics and becoming confident in one's own ability. It is important, therefore, that we continually monitor and assess our students' attitudes and beliefs.

WHAT ARE IMPORTANT ATTITUDES TOWARD MATHEMATICS AND LEARNING?

Attitudes reflect how we react or relate to mathematics. They affect the way we behave. The picture in **figure 2.14** describes some of the positive and negative attitudes toward mathematics that teachers have found in their middle school students.

FIG. 2.14

A BATTERY OF ATTITUDES TOWARD MATHEMATICS

A Battery of Attitudes

+	−
enjoy	avoid
value	dislike
like	anxious
confident	dread
eager	lack of confidence
persistent	stress
comfortable	unmotivated
enthusiastic	not interested
motivated	

Assessing Attitudes and Beliefs

WHAT ARE COMMON BELIEFS ABOUT MATHEMATICS AND LEARNING?

Beliefs describe how we think about things. Middle school students have had ample opportunities in elementary school to develop pretty strong beliefs about mathematics and how it is learned. The following list describes some of the beliefs that middle and high school students have about mathematics and problem solving:

Middle school students believe that—

■ *Mathematics is computation.*

■ *Mathematics problems should be quickly solvable in just a few steps.*

■ *The goal of doing mathematics is to obtain "right answers."*

■ *The role of the mathematics student is to receive mathematical knowledge and demonstrate that it has been received.*

■ *The role of the mathematics teacher is to transmit mathematical knowledge and to verify that students have received this knowledge. (Frank 1988)*

High school students believe that—

■ *Almost all mathematics problems can be solved by the direct application of the facts, rules, formulas, and procedures shown by the teacher or given in the textbook.*

■ *Mathematics textbook exercises can be solved only by the methods presented in the book.*

■ *Only the mathematics to be tested is important and worth knowing.*

■ *Mathematics is created by very prodigious and creative people; other people just try to learn what is handed down. (Garofalo 1989)*

READ ABOUT...

■ *For more reading about assessing attitudes and beliefs, read "Assessing Students' Dispositions: Using Journals to Improve Students' Performance" by Theresa Bagley (1992), "Exploring and Changing Visions of Mathematics Teaching and Learning: What Do Students Think?" by Jayne Fleener, Gloria Dupree, and Larry Craven (1997), and "Assessing Students' Beliefs" by Denise Spangler (1992).*

Assessing Attitudes and Beliefs

HOW DO I MONITOR AND ASSESS ATTITUDES AND BELIEFS?

Many teachers have had success in monitoring their students' feelings and thoughts about mathematics through daily or weekly journals. Read the two students' journal entries in **figures 2.15** and **2.16** and think about what they tell us about these students.

FIG. 2.15

JOURNAL ENTRY ABOUT ATTITUDES

> Mathematics puts everything in perspective; that there are some situations where not even the smartest people in the world can figure out and, most importantly, understand Yet, on the other hand there is a definate and exact answer to other situations. That's what math is; the mystery and continuation of symbols, numbers, and anything that has to do with figuring that will us everyday in life, no matter what we do for a living. We'd be no where without math.

FIG. 2.16

JOURNAL ENTRY ABOUT BELIEFS

> Mathematics is the study of numerical problems and equations. There are many parts to math like subtraction. addition, division, multiplication, Algebra, geometry and many others. For each one of these listed above there are different rules to solve each problem or equation. Many of the rules are simple but others are more complex. Mathematics is a very important tool to know especially when you progress to higher levels and when choosing a career. I feel mathematics is the study and rules to solve different problems and equations. I feel it is very important ~~ana~~ a skill that everyone needs to know No matter if it comes easy or hard.

CHAPTER 2

An Assessment Toolbox

WHAT ARE MY ASSESSMENT CHOICES?

We will now describe six different assessment tools that can be used in the mathematics classroom. For each tool, we will—

- describe what the tool is best designed to do;

- explain what the tool is good for;

- offer samples of students' work;

- provide references to other resources.

As we begin to use more assessment tools, it is helpful to think about the strengths and limitations of each tool. Which tools provide the best evidence of a student's proficiency with skills? Are there some assessment tools that just do not give good evidence of problem solving? How many different tools do I need to gather evidence of what a student has achieved at the completion of a term?

It is also useful to think about assessment tools in terms of important questions they help to answer.

As part of ongoing instruction—

- Do my students understand the mathematics that I expect them to understand?

- What instructional shifts should I make today or tomorrow or this week to improve understanding?

At the conclusion of instruction—

- What have my students achieved?

- How will I modify this lesson or unit the next time I teach it?

These questions address the different purposes of assessment and help us select the appropriate assessment tool or tools described in **figure 2.17** on the following page.

An Assessment Toolbox

FIG. 2.17

PICTURE OF AN ASSESSMENT TOOLBOX

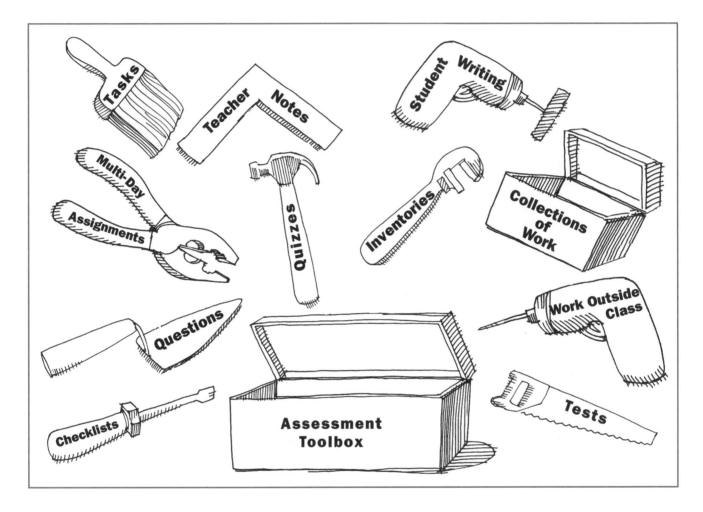

CHAPTER *2*

Quizzes and Tests

WHAT ARE THEY?

Quizzes and tests, the icons of mathematics assessment for years, have important roles. Tests and quizzes, in addition to being end-of-unit assessments, can also be pretests at the beginning of a unit. They may also be used periodically during a unit or chapter (for example, "weekly quizzes"). We often use them to measure individual achievement in a time-limited setting. Depending on our purpose, quizzes and tests may be given to individual students or to groups of students.

WHAT ARE THEY GOOD FOR?

Well-constructed quizzes and tests—

- tell us how students perform when they have had the chance to prepare and study;
- allow students who do not speak up in class to excel and show understanding;
- give us a way to pose particular questions to all our students at once;
- permit every student (not just the ones we are able to call on in class discussion) to construct their own response;
- are particularly effective in assessing skills proficiency, understanding, and, to a lesser extent, problem solving.

HOW CAN I USE TESTS AND QUIZZES TO IMPROVE STUDENT PERFORMANCE?

Tests and quizzes can be used to help students understand their own performance. The work in **figures 2.18** and **2.19** comes from a sixth-grade mathematics classroom. The teacher gives challenging quizzes frequently during a unit of instruction. The students employ these quizzes to check their ability to use the concepts and skills in the unit. What is important, from the students' viewpoint, is to correct their mistakes and to make sure they understand any troublesome concepts or skills on the quiz.

FIG. 2.18

SAMPLE QUIZ CORRECTIONS

Math °6
1-13-97

Quiz Corrections

(4) problem: 8^5 answer: 8x8x8
(5) problem: 5^2 answer: 5x5
(8) problem: 10^4 answer: 10,000
(9) problem: 7^2 answer: 49
(11) problem: 3x3 answer: 3^2
(14) problem: one million answer: 10^6
(15) problem: 128 answer: 1.28×10^2
(16) problem: 36 answer: $.36 \times 10^2$

FIG. 2.19

SAMPLE QUIZ

EXPONENTS QUIZ #2

I. Match the left column with the right column.

1. 2^4 C — A. 3 X 2
2. 4^2 D — B. 8
3. 3^2 E — C. two to the fourth power
4. 2^3 B — D. four to the second power
E. 9

II. Write each number with exponents.

5. 6,000,000 6×10^6
6. 9000 9×10^3
7. 350,000 35×10^4
8. one million —
9. 8 X 8 X 8 X 8 X 8 8^5
10. 10 X 10 X 10 10^3
11. 16 16×10^1

III. Multiply. Leave in exponent form.

12. $10^2 \times 10^3$ 100x1,000=100,000
13. $10^5 \times 10^2$ 100,000x100=10,000,000
14. $(9 \times 10^7) \times (11 \times 10^3)$ 99×10^{10}
15. $(7 \times 10^2) \times (4 \times 10^4)$ 28×10^6
16. $(3 \times 10^3) \times (8 \times 10^3)$ 24×10^6

IV. Evaluate. (Find the answer)

17. 8^2 16
18. 10^5 100,000

Quizzes and Tests

FIG. 2.20

STUDENT-CONSTRUCTED TEST (PAGE 1)

The following test was produced by Jeremy's class of Year 9 pupils:

1) Find the equation for lines **A**, **B**, and **C**.

2) In general, how do you find the equation from the graph?

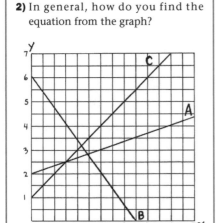

READ ABOUT...

■ *Read about a teacher who used students' self-assessment in her mathematics class in "Students as Assessors" in* Mathematics Assessment: Cases and Discussion Questions for Grades K–5 *(Bush 2001).*

HOW CAN I INVOLVE MY STUDENTS IN CONSTRUCTING QUIZZES AND TESTS?

Involving students in constructing tests and quizzes has proven to be a successful assessment tool for some teachers. Students in an eighth-grade class constructed the test in **figures 2.20** and **2.21**. This assessment was part of the "Awareness of Learning" project, in which middle-grades teachers evaluated self-assessment methods they had devised and used in their own classrooms. Teachers announced that the test was to be put together from a student-created "question bank." Students worked as partners to write questions without relying on their textbooks. The teacher assembled the test from the bank of questions. Questions included sample "full credit" solutions.

FIG. 2.21

STUDENT-CONSTRUCTED TEST (PAGE 2)

3) Find the relationship in these sets of numbers and add another pair to the set:

A	B
1	1
2	7
4	19
6	31
10	55

4) Describe in not more than 50 words the definition of *inverse*.

5) Find the relationship:

C	D
–1	3
5	39
–5	–21
0	9
2	21

6) Given this rule, $4x - 2$, describe the numbers which go with **a)** 3   **b)** 6   **c)** 10

7) Find the equation of this line

8) Give an example of: **a)** a positive gradient
b) a negative gradient
c) a zero gradient

Draw the lines on the same set of axes.

CHAPTER 2

Work Outside Class

WHAT IS IT?

These assessments include homework and "problems of the week" (POW). Some teachers give POWs to students on Monday to be handed in on Friday because students may need several days—to think about and come back to the problem, to collect information, or to try a second or third approach—before coming to a satisfying solution.

WHAT IS IT GOOD FOR?

Outside class assessments give students the chance to apply concepts or skills. They allow students to do extended, independent work involving problem solving. These assessments give us evidence of students' perseverance and responsibility. They also give evidence of concentration and follow-through, especially for students who are slow to get started on an assignment. Work done outside class also allows us to monitor students' progress and measure students' achievement for extended tasks.

A fifth-and-sixth-grade teacher gave the following problem to her class to do as a "problem of the week."

Tetherball Tournament

Beth, Cesar, Nora, Roy, Steven, and Joanna want to plan a tetherball tournament on Saturday. The players have just one tetherball court to use. During the tournament, each player will play a match with each of the other players. A match takes 15 minutes. How long will the tetherball tournament take from start to finish? Explain or show how you figured out your answer.

Work Outside Class

FIG. 2.22

STUDENT WORK #1— TETHERBALL TOURNAMENT

This class had done some work with patterns (function machines and square numbers) as well as some work with combinations. The teacher saw this problem as one that integrates skills, concepts, and problem solving. This teacher also included a general set of instructions to encourage clear communication. The student work is shown in **figures 2.22, 2.23,** and **2.24.** Note how different the students' responses are. Also note how detailed the teacher's analyses are.

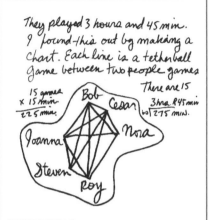

RESPONSE A
Teacher's analysis:

This student uses a representation in which each line from one player to another represents a game played. An advantage of this representation is its clarity about the reciprocal nature of "playing a game": the fact that every player plays the same number of games is immediately apparent from the representation. A disadvantage of this representation is that it is hard to keep track of large numbers. The student's use of division to regroup 225 minutes into 3 hours, 45 minutes is accurate and clear.

FIG. 2.23

STUDENT WORK #2—TETHERBALL TOURNAMENT

RESPONSE B
Teacher's analysis:

This student uses a chart to keep accurate track of the number of games played. The total number of minutes for the games in each column is shown, then added across to get a total of 225 minutes. This total is not converted to hours and minutes, as it would ordinarily be for this situation. To address this, ask the student, "How many hours and minutes is 225 minutes?" There is also confusing communication whether the children in the task each play the same number of games. To address this, ask, "How many minutes does each student spend actually playing tetherball?"

READ ABOUT...

■ *For more resources for work outside class, look at "Problems of the Week" by Lyle Fisher and Bill Midagovich (1981), and "101 Short Problems" edited by Jean Stenmark (1995).*

FIG. 2.24

STUDENT WORK #3—TETHERBALL TOURNAMENT

RESPONSE C
Teacher's analysis:

This student organizes a matrix that is easy to extend and that can show very effectively how triangular numbers increase. The student, however, makes an error which leads him to a solution of exactly twice the correct number of games. He correctly enters "0" for the boxes in which the row and column for a single player intersect. He has filled in the matrix, though, as if "A plays B" were a different game than one in which "B plays A." Once the student understands that "A plays B/B plays A" is a single, reciprocal event, the 15 games in the matrix will illustrate the triangular number pattern literally—with a triangle.

CHAPTER 2

Figures 2.22, 2.23, and 2.24 are reprinted with permission from the California Mathematics Council—Teachers, Administrators, and Parents Dedicated to Quality Mathematics Education.

Multiday Assignments

WHAT ARE THEY?

These assessments are longer pieces of work—often ones which require work both inside and outside of the classroom. They may be based on assignments that are the same for the whole class.

WHAT ARE THEY GOOD FOR?

Multiday assignments give students a chance to do work that looks like doing "real mathematics," the mathematics that adults do. In doing a multiday assignment, students must often plan their time, locate and use resources, decide how to test their ideas, decide whether and how to modify their approach to a question or problem, interpret the results they get, and decide how to generalize solutions. Sometimes, students may have to make the initial decision about which interesting mathematics questions they choose to pursue without guidance from the teacher.

This type of assessment is very motivational, especially if students can choose their own area of interest, develop the plan, and produce a report or exhibition as a finished product. For this reason, the finished products make excellent displays in the halls of middle schools or in local businesses, science centers, or malls.

We must, however, exercise caution with these types of assessment. Mathematics problems that arise outside the classroom sometimes cause equity problems. That is, not all students may have access to the resources to complete the multiday assignments. The following is a list of possible areas of investigation for multiday assignments appropriate for middle school students that has been compiled by the New Standards Project.

New Standards Areas for Investigation—

- *a data study based on civic, economic, or social issues;*

- *a mathematical model of a physical phenomena often used in science projects;*

- *the design of a physical structure;*

- *a pure mathematics investigation.*

Multiday Assignments

WHAT ARE SOME EXAMPLES?

Some multiday assignments are more appropriate for groups of students. The assignment below was given to groups of sixth graders:

Each of you will collect data on the head size of fourth, fifth, and sixth graders and make a recommendation to a company that wants to sell hats to ten-to-twelve-year-olds. They want to know which three sizes (in centimeters) will fit the broadest range of children, and what proportion to order of each size.

Some multiday assignments like the one below are more appropriate for individual students:

Student: I noticed that some numbers such as "9" and "10" can be the sum of consecutive numbers. You can get 9 by adding 4 and 5; you can get 10 by adding 1, 2, 3, and 4. I wonder if there are more numbers that have consecutive addends or more numbers that don't. I also wonder if there are patterns to help predict whether or not a number will have them. My teacher said that these were good questions to investigate.

The **Mountain Bike Project** provides an excellent example of a multiday assignment. **Figures 2.25** and **2.26** illustrate the specific information provided to the students working on the project.

FIG. 2.25

MOUNTAIN BIKE PROJECT (PAGE 1)

Pre-Assessment   Group Page 1
Data Sense

Mountain Bikes

How the bikes were rated—*Mountain Bike Quarterly*

Brand and Model: These are the latest model mountain and road bikes.

Price: Manufacturer's suggested retail price.

Weight: Tested bikes with a 19- or 20-inch frame (weight in pounds).

Shifting ease: How easy the bike can be put into gear while riding. Rated on a five-point scale (5 4 3 2 1) with 5 being the easiest.

Brakes Dry or Wet: How quickly each bicycle was able to make a panic stop from 15 mph using both brakes. Rated on a five-point scale (5 4 3 2 1) with 5 being the quickest.

Brake Control: How quickly and evenly the brakes responded. Rated on a five-point scale (5 4 3 2 1) with 5 being the best.

Handling (on-road and off-road): Each bike was tested through a series of maneuvers in both on-road and off-road conditions. Rated on a five-point scale (5 4 3 2 1) with 5 being the best.

Shock absorption: Each bike was tested by riding the bike along a 48-foot "ladder" at about 7 mph and judging how severely the bumps were felt through the seat and handlebars. Rated on a five point scale (5 4 3 2 1) with 5 being the best.

Coasting: Each bike was tested by coasting down a steep downhill section of road for a half mile. Rated on a five-point scale (5 4 3 2 1) with 5 being the best.

Saddle comfort: Men and women testers made this judgment after riding the bikes along the 48 foot ladder. Rated on a five-point scale (5 4 3 2 1) with 5 being the best.

Gear range: A wide gear range means a more versatile bike.

CHAPTER 2

Multiday Assignments

FIG. 2.26

MOUNTAIN BIKE PROJECT (PAGE 2)

Pre-Assessment   Group Page 2
Data Sense
Mountain Bikes

Available Frame Sizes: The smallest and largest frames offered. Manufacturers typically make frames in two-inch increments

Brand and Model	Price $	Weight lbs.	Shifting Ease	Brakes Dry	Brakes Wet3	Braking Control
Bianchi Boardwalk	414	29	4	5	3	4
Cannondale SH400	479	28.5	5	4	4	5
Diamond Black	264	33.25	3	5	5	4
Giant Innova	370	27.5	4	4	4	3
Miyata Triple Cross	425	28.75	4	4	3	3
Nishiki Saga	510	27.75	5	4	3	5
Peugeot Limestone	350	31.5	4	5	4	4
Raleigh Eclipse CX	262	31	3	4	3	4
Ross Mt. Olympus XC	260	30	3	4	3	2
Schwinn Crisscross	310	29	5	4	2	5
Specialized Crossroads	350	28.5	4	5	2	2
Trek Mult-Track 720	411	30	5	3	3	5
Univega Activa-ES	270	30.5	3	5	3	4

Brand and Model	On-Road Handling	Off-Road Handling	Shock Absrp.	Coasting	Saddle Comfort	Gear Range Low/High	Frame Size
Bianchi Boardwalk	3	3	4	4	2	27/108	15.5–23
Cannondale SH400	3	3	1	3	3	25/104	19–25
Diamond Black	2	4	5	2	2	26/89	15.5–22
Giant Innova	4	2	3	2	2	24/96	15.5–23.5
Miyata Triple Cross	2	3	4	5	2	25/100	18–25
Nishiki Saga	3	2	1	5	1	24/96	16–22
Peugeot Limestone	3	3	3	5	5	27/108	18–24
Raleigh Eclipse CX	3	3	3	4	3	27/108	18–24
Ross Mt. Olympus XC	2	3	3	2	2	27/93	19.5–23
Schwinn Crisscross	2	4	4	3	3	27/100	18–22
Specialized Crossroads	3	3	4	3	3	25/100	16.5–22
Trek Mult-Track 720	3	3	3	4	2	25/100	17–23
Univega Activa-ES	2	3	3	3	4	27/93	16.5–22.5

Eighth graders were asked to use data about different models of mountain bikes in several ways over a two-week period. One of the main questions students addressed appears in the following box.

Mountain Bike Project

On the basis of the information shown in an issue of *Mountain Bike Quarterly* (where thirteen makes and models were given ratings of 1–5 in each of nine categories), determine whether "price" and "quality rating" are positively correlated?

Multiday Assignments

READ ABOUT...

■ *Read about a seventh-grade teacher's attempt to assess a multiday geometry assignment in "Tessellation Presentation" in* Mathematics Assessment: Cases and Discussion Questions for Grades 6–12 *(Bush 2000).*

RESOURCES

The following resources provide examples of good multiday assignments for middle school students: "Assessment as a Dialogue: A Means of Interacting with Middle School Students" by Kris Warloe (1993) and the New Standards Project, Center for Education and the Economy, Washington, D.C.

Figures 2.27 and 2.28 illustrate one student's work on this assignment.

FIG. 2.27

STUDENT WORK—MOUNTAIN BIKE MEAN SCORES

MEAN SCORES OF MOUNTAIN BIKE RATINGS

NAME OF BIKE		CALCULATIONS	MEAN
Bianchi Boardwalk	$414	$\frac{32}{9} = 3.55$	3.6
Cannondale SH400	$479	$\frac{31}{9} = 3.44$	3.4
Diamond Back	$254	$\frac{32}{9} = 3.55$	3.6
Giant Innova	$370	$\frac{28}{9} = 3.11$	3.1
Miyata Triple Cross	$425	$\frac{30}{9} = 3.33$	3.3
Nishiki Saga	$510	$\frac{29}{9} = 3.22$	3.2
Peugeot Limestone	$350	$\frac{36}{9} = 4$	4.0
Raleigh Eclipse CX	$262	$\frac{30}{9} = 3.33$	3.3
Ross Mt. Olympus XC	$260	$\frac{24}{9} = 2.66$	2.7
Schwinn Crisscross	$310	$\frac{32}{9} = 3.55$	3.6
Specialized Crossroad	$350	$\frac{29}{9} = 3.22$	3.2
Trek Multi-Track 720	$411	$\frac{31}{9} = 3.44$	3.4
Univega Activa-ES	$270	$\frac{30}{9} = 3.33$	3.3

The student constructed the table on a computer, then wrote in the prices for the thirteen models. Next, he showed the calculations that led to the mean rating (each of the nine features was given equal weight). He then constructed a scatterplot to graph price against the mean rating for each of the thirteen bikes. What conclusions might the student draw from his graph?

Multiday Assignments

FIG. 2.28

STUDENT WORK—MOUNTAIN BIKE RATING VS. PRICE

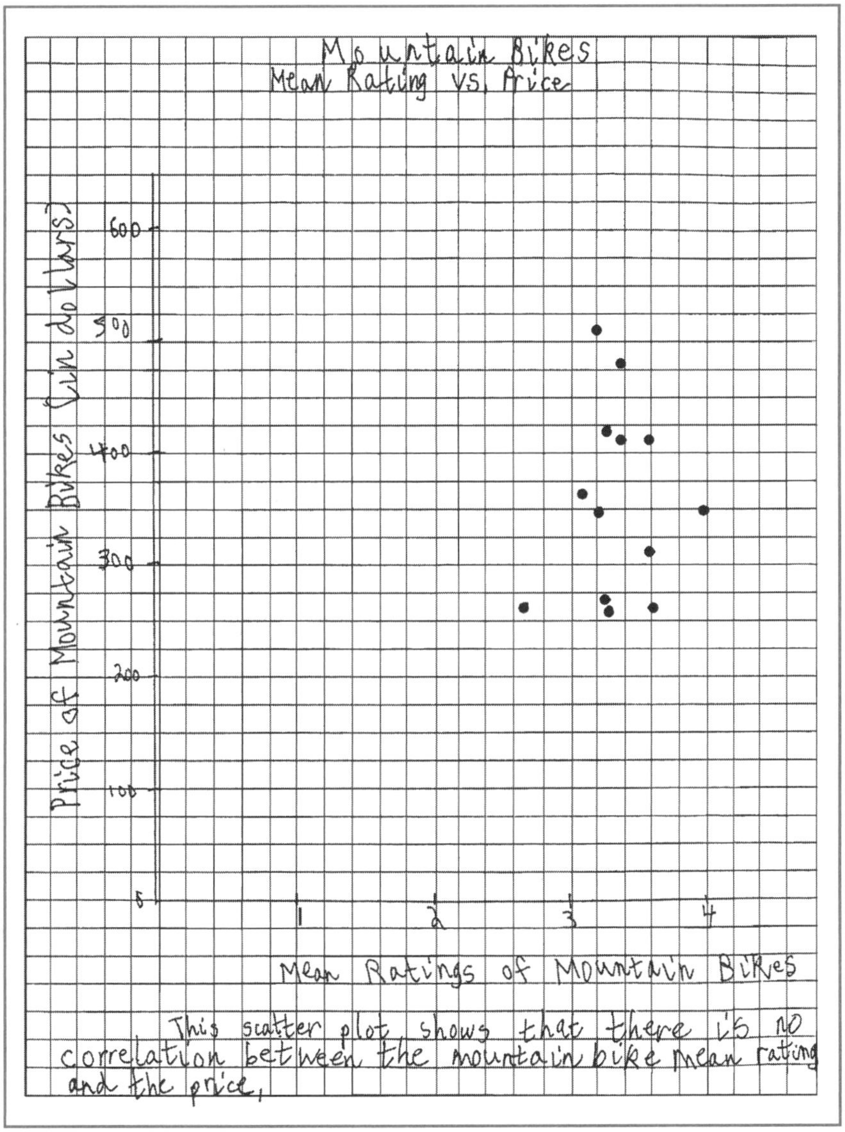

Mountain Bikes
Mean Rating vs. Price

Price of Mountain Bikes (in dollars)

600
500
400
300
200
100
0

1   2   3   4

Mean Ratings of Mountain Bikes

This scatter plot shows that there is no correlation between the mountain bike mean rating and the price.

Teacher Notes and Checklists

WHAT ARE THEY?

Teacher notes and checklists are assessment tools that are often used during instruction to note the results of observations or interviews. Notes and checklists record evidence about individual students during teaching. Though these assessments may not always be planned, they often yield useful information about students.

WHAT ARE THEY GOOD FOR?

Teacher notes and checklists tell us—

■ how students think, what they say, and what they do about mathematics during routine activities;

■ how students whose written work is weak figure things out;

■ how students use skills and understanding in solving problems.

WHAT ARE SOME EXAMPLES?

Figures 2.29 and **2.30** illustrate two checklists, each focusing on a different student behavior. The first looks at how students work in groups. The second checklist focuses on assessing students' understanding.

FIG. 2.29

CHECKLIST FOR GROUP WORK

FIGURE 6						
Cooperative-learning checklist						
Skills / NAMES						
Followed directions	❑	❑	❑	❑	❑	❑
Stayed on task	❑	❑	❑	❑	❑	❑
Explained ideas clearly to others	❑	❑	❑	❑	❑	❑
Supported ideas of others	❑	❑	❑	❑	❑	❑
Developed a plan	❑	❑	❑	❑	❑	❑
Engaged in constructive criticism	❑	❑	❑	❑	❑	❑
Persisted in completing the assignment	❑	❑	❑	❑	❑	❑
Performed the following roles:						
Checker	❑	❑	❑	❑	❑	❑
Recorder	❑	❑	❑	❑	❑	❑
Leader	❑	❑	❑	❑	❑	❑
Summarizer	❑	❑	❑	❑	❑	❑

CHAPTER 2

From Cross, Lee, and Michael C. Hynes "Assessing Mathematics Learning for Students with Learning Differences." *Arithmetic Teacher* 41 (March 1994): 375.

Teacher Notes and Checklists

FIG. 2.30

CHECKLIST FOR UNDERSTANDING

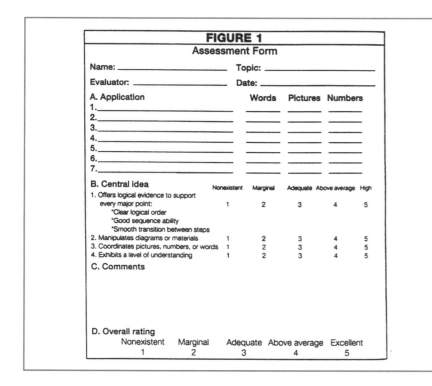

From Stix, Andi. "Pic-Jour Math: Pictorial Journal Writing in Mathematics." *Arithmetic Teacher* 41 (January 1994): 265.

Figure 2.31 illustrates a set of teacher notes written by a teacher over a period of several months. These notes were written on labels and attached on a page designated for each student.

READal ABOUT...

■ *For additional reading about teacher notes and checklists, read "Assessment Through Classroom Observation" in* Assessment Alternatives in Mathematics, *edited by David Clarke (1988); "Valuing What We See" by Doug Clarke and Linda Wilson (1994); and* Mathematics Assessment: Myths, Models, Good Questions, and Practical Suggestions, *edited by Jean Stenmark (1991).*

■ *See Chapter 3 to learn more about conducting effective observations and interviews.*

■ *Read about a teacher's struggle with observations in "On the Job Learning" in* Mathematics Assessment: Cases and Discussion Questions for Grades K–5 *(Bush 2001).*

FIG. 2.31

TEACHER NOTES

Student Writing and Inventories

FIG. 2.32

JOURNAL ENTRY 1

> I like math! I do; though I think that "busy-work" is very boring. I like math because of the challenge of solving difficult problems. After solving a difficult problem I feel good and want to take on another one. Math can make me feel as though I have conquered something previously unknown, and it feels great! Mathematics can give you power that you can use in the "real" world. A power over numbers. A power to get a good job and so much more. It is the one thing that all a nearly all jobs use in the entire world! Math is power, and Everyone should use it.

FIG. 2.33

JOURNAL ENTRY 2

> I know, and I am pretty sure that most people know that math is extremely important. But I really dislike it. I think there is too much repetition in math. When I understand something I really don't want to do 40 problems that will just take up time. I have never really liked math from the start. I think I began to bore easier as life goes on. I would prefer writing a beautifully crafted Essay or learning about the collinization and independance of America. Although I realize the importance, I dislike math.

WHAT ARE THEY?

Writing assignments and inventories are assessments that are produced by students, rather than teachers. They challenge students to think about their mathematical strengths and weaknesses, their attitudes, or their beliefs. They often take the form of student journals, students' reflections on their thinking and methods of working, and student-completed inventories.

WHAT ARE THEY GOOD FOR?

By actively involving students in the assessment process, student writing and inventories—

- encourage students to think about how they solved a problem or performed a skill;

- help students view their accomplishments in terms of their own strengths and areas for improvement;

- give students ways to think consciously about expanding their mathematical repertoire: types of strategies, use of representations, focus on content areas;

- provide us with evidence that students use concepts and problem-solving strategies.

WHAT ARE SOME EXAMPLES?

Figures 2.32 and 2.33 provide journal entries written by middle school students. What do these journal entries tell us about these two students?

In **Figure 2.34** is a student's explanation of his thinking about a problem. How would you rate the problem-solving ability of this student? Why?

CHAPTER *2*

Student Writing and Inventories

FIGURE 2.34

EXPLANATION OF PROBLEM SOLVING

Individual Worksheet

1. How did you conduct your activity? We conducted our activity by making a multiplication table with numbers 1-6. We then counted the odd products and the even products. We got 9 odd and 27 even. We then decided to find out the percentage. 9/27 = 33%. Subtracted 33 from 100 to see what our percentage was for an even number and it was 67%.

2. What were the results of your activity? The result was that the chances of rolling an odd number was far less than rolling an even number. And that although you role and odd products it's doubble the even points.

3. Is the game fair? Explain your reasoning using the results of your activity.

Yes. I think it's fair because even if the chances of rolling an odd product is very little comparing to the even percentage the points are double the even points.

4. Is there a fairer way to award points for this game? Explain your reasoning.

No. Because the game is fair with the amount of points. You have already given. You could make the points a bit larger just as long as the odds points are 1 more than the even points.

Student Writing and Inventories

SOMETHING TO THINK ABOUT

Journal entries may be free writing or stimulated by specific prompts from teachers. Which do you prefer? Why?

Inventories are also useful tools in providing evidence about students and helping students assess themselves. The inventory in **figure 2.35** is one example of the many used by teachers.

FIG. 2.35

QUESTIONNAIRE FOR STUDENT SELF-ASSESSMENT

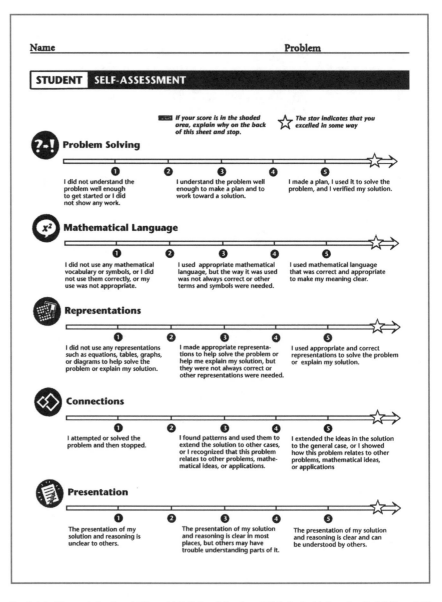

Reprinted with permission from McDougal Littell, Inc. Taken from *Middle Grades Mathematics, Book 2* (Copyright ©1998) written by Rick Billstein and Jim Williamson.

Collections of Work

WHAT ARE THEY?

Collections of work include portfolios, work folders, and other mathematical work collected for a specific reason. Teachers may compile them themselves, have students compile them, or both. How the collection looks and what is in it depends on its purpose. A collection of work may take in a single unit of study, or it may span a number of years of the student's mathematical education.

WHAT ARE THEY GOOD FOR?

Depending on how they are used, collections of work—

- provide evidence of students' use of skills, concepts, and problem solving in a variety of situations;

- show a student's mathematical growth over a period of time;

- involve students in a "draft and revise" approach to doing mathematical work and model how mathematics work is often done outside school;

- enable students who persevere to have the opportunity to display their effort;

- give students responsibility for organizing their own learning;

- provide educators, parents and other caregivers, and students with a picture of accomplishment.

Entries in the students' collections of work often include examples of the other assessment tools described in this section. Much of what distinguishes portfolios or other collections of work from random sets of assignments is a set of organizing principles that underlie them.

READ ABOUT...

■ *Read about a primary teacher's attempt to incorporate mathematics portfolios in her assessment practices in* "Developing a Portfolio Culture" in Mathematics Assessment: Cases and Discussion Questions for Grades K–5 *(Bush 2001).*

■ *For more reading about using collections of work to assess, read* "Student Mathematics Portfolio: More Than a Display Case" by Mary Crowley (1993), "Portfolio Assessment: Making It Work the First Time" by Teresa Kuhs (1994), "Planning for Classroom Portfolio Assessment" by Diana Lambdin and Vicki Walker (1994), and Mathematics Assessment: Myths, Models, Good Questions, and Practical Suggestions, *edited by Jean Stenmark (1991).*

Collections of Work

WHAT IS AN EXAMPLE?

The sample in the next few pages is taken from the New Standards middle-grades mathematics portfolio. The organizing principle of the portfolio is a set of exhibits of a student's best work. The New Standards portfolio is designed to be viewed and scored by the student's teacher as well as other outside readers. In **figures 2.36, 2.37, 2.38,** and **2.39** are the purposes and requirements of the New Standards portfolios.

FIG. 2.36

PURPOSE AND REQUIREMENTS OF A NEW STANDARDS™ PORTFOLIO
CONCEPTUAL UNDERSTANDING EXHIBIT

CONCEPTUAL UNDERSTANDING EXHIBIT

Purpose

The purpose of this exhibit is to show how well you understand and can use important mathematical concepts. How do you know when you understand a concept?

■ **You can use the concept** in problems where you have been taught to use it. You show a deeper understanding when you can recognize when to use the concept in a non-routine or unfamiliar situation.

■ **You can represent the concept in many ways.** For example, you can use algebraic symbols, labeled diagrams, graphs, tables, charts, and verbal descriptions.

■ **You can explain the concept to someone else.** Explaining a concept involves showing how it's used, how it's represented, and how it relates to other math concepts.

Exhibit Requirements

Prepare four entries, one in each of these areas of mathematics: Number and Operation, Geometry and Measurement, Functions and Algebra, Probability and Statistics. Attach the appropriate slip for each entry. Each entry should include at least one, but no more than two problems that show how you used and represented the concepts. Entries can include:

■ problems that require explanations

■ problems of the week

■ assignments to explain and illustrate a concept to someone else

■ investigations of a mathematical question

Your entries must show how you can use a concept, represent it in different ways, and explain it. Use a combination of words, diagrams, graphs, tables, and charts.

> **NOTE: Sometimes a portfolio will include work from three years of middle school mathematics. Most portfolios have work from only one year. If this is your situation, your entries will probably show more depth in your course area. A good course, however, will integrate a broad range of mathematical topics. Please do your best to include an entry for each area of mathematics.**

Figures 2.36, 2.37, and 2.38 are reprinted with permission from New Standards™. The New Standards™ assessment system includes performance standards with performance descriptions, student work samples and commentaries, on-demand examinations, and a portfolio system. For more information contact the National Center on Education and the Economy, 202-783-3668 or www.ncee.org.

CHAPTER 2

Collections of Work

FIG. 2.37

PURPOSE AND REQUIREMENTS OF THE NEW STANDARDS™ PORTFOLIO—SKILLS AND COMMUNICATION EXHIBIT

SKILLS AND COMMUNICATION EXHIBIT

Purpose

The purpose of this exhibit is to show your mathematical skills and how well you communicate mathematically.

Exhibit Requirements

Separate pieces of work are not required for the Skills and Communication Exhibit. Entries submitted for the first three exhibits may be sufficient. If not, a few additional pieces of work may be included here to fill important gaps.

There are two entry slips, one for skills and one for communication. On these entry slips, write down where to find evidence of your mathematical skills and ability to communicate mathematically.

If you want to demonstrate a particular skill or communicate mathematical ideas in other ways, attach the additional pieces of work to the appropriate entry slips for this exhibit.

FIG. 2.38

PURPOSE AND REQUIREMENTS OF THE NEW STANDARDS™ PORTFOLIO—PROBLEM-SOLVING EXHIBIT

PROBLEM-SOLVING EXHIBIT

Purpose

The purpose of this exhibit is to show how good a problem solver you are. Select problems that show how well you formulate, solve, and draw conclusions.

■ **Problem Formulation** You formulate the mathematical question(s) needed to solve the problem.

■ **Problem Implementation** You organize the information, solution strategies, use of mathematical concepts, execution of your methods, and reasoning techniques.

■ **Problem Conclusion** You explain why your conclusion(s) make sense. In addition, you go beyond the problem to generalize the result to other situations.

Exhibit Requirements

There is one entry in the Problem-Solving Exhibit. This entry is a collection of four problems.

Prepare the entry and attach the entry slip to it. Select four different kinds of problems. They should show that you can use a variety of mathematical concepts, skills, and strategies to solve them. Across the problems, you should also demonstrate problem formulation, implementation, and conclusion.

Exhibit Requirements (cont.)

When you select problems for this exhibit, look for:

■ problems that show a thoughtful strategy rather than a direct application of known concepts

■ problems that show a systematic plan for dealing with a situation

■ problems that involve mathematical modeling of real world situations

■ problems with a definite solution but many possible routes to the solution

■ problems that investigate an unfamiliar situation in mathematics

■ problems that require you to extend a known concept to new situations not previously studied

Prepare each problem so that anybody can understand what you were trying to accomplish. Show how you worked through the problem, and explain why your conclusion(s) make sense.

Collections of Work

FIG. 2.39

PURPOSE AND REQUIREMENTS OF THE NEW STANDARDS™ PORTFOLIO PROJECT EXHIBIT

PROJECT EXHIBIT

Purpose

The purpose of this exhibit is to show how you put mathematics to work in a project over an extended period of time. A project needs a balance of the different ways of presenting information and ideas. A balanced presentation uses representations such as charts, diagrams, maps, formulas, equations, calculations, and graphs. It uses verbal explanations to clarify how the representations relate to one another. Projects typically include:

- a question, objective, or plan

- a description of the methods used and how the project was carried out

- a mathematical analysis of the results and a general application of the findings

- a presentation or report of the conclusions

Exhibit Requirements

Prepare one entry for the Project Exhibit. Your project should involve research and applications of mathematics over a period of at least three weeks. Attach the appropriate entry slip to the work. If you substitute a different kind of project, make up an entry slip to explain what you were trying to accomplish.

Select one from the following kinds of projects:

- **Data Study** Carry out a study of data related to current civic, economic, or social issues. Use statistical measures to generalize from the data. For example, you might gather and analyze data from your neighborhood and compare it to published statistics for your city, state, or nation.

Exhibit Requirements (cont.)

- **Mathematical Modeling** Carry out a study of a physical system. Create a mathematical model that uses functions to show how one variable depends on another. Show how the mathematical functions represent the relationships in the physical system. For example, you might compare the growth of a group of plants under a variety of conditions, e.g., different amounts of water, fertilizer, exposure to sunlight.

- **Design of a Physical Structure** Create a design for a physical structure. Use geometry and measurement to give realistic specifications for the design. For example, you might work with a limited budget to design a recreational space that is situated on an acre of land. Your design might include a building and some recreational equipment in sizes appropriate for the space.

- **Management and Planning** Carry out a study of a situation involving issues such as costs/benefits, risks, and trade-offs. Analyze the different choices and make generalizations across different conditions. For example, you might make up a schedule of practices and other events in the school gymnasium, taking into account home and away games and boys' and girls' teams.

- **Pure Mathematical Investigation** Carry out a mathematical investigation of an idea in pure mathematics. Use methods of logic and proof to make generalizations. For example, you might investigate the numbers in Pascal's triangle and describe the relationships among them.

- **History of a Mathematical Idea** Carry out a historical study tracing the development of a mathematical concept and the people who contributed to it. For example, you might investigate the concept of x and its importance in mathematics.

Reprinted with permission from New Standards™. The New Standards™ assessment system includes performance standards with performance descriptions, student work samples and commentaries, on-demand examinations, and a portfolio system. For more information contact the National Center on Education and the Economy, 202-783-3668 or www.ncee.org.

CHAPTER *2*

Collections of Work

Figures **2.40**, **2.41**, and **2.42** provide entries of the New Standards portfolio from one student.

FIG. 2.40

NEW STANDARDS™ PORTFOLIO (PAGE 1)

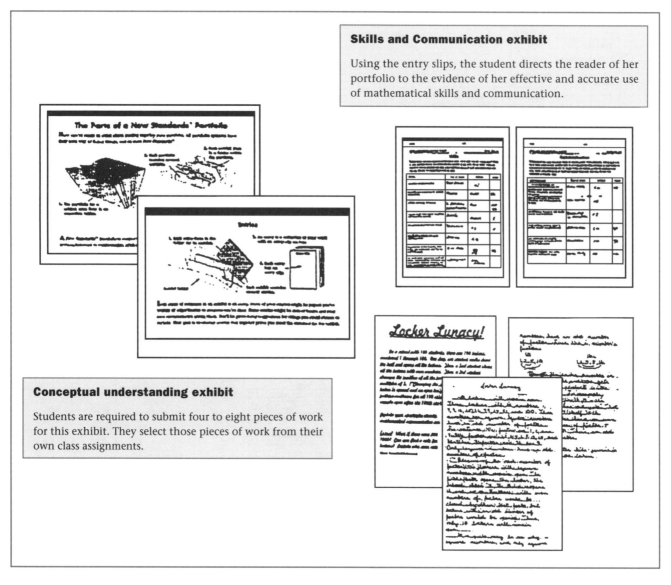

Skills and Communication exhibit

Using the entry slips, the student directs the reader of her portfolio to the evidence of her effective and accurate use of mathematical skills and communication.

Conceptual understanding exhibit

Students are required to submit four to eight pieces of work for this exhibit. They select those pieces of work from their own class assignments.

Collections of Work

FIG. 2.41

NEW STANDARDS™ PORTFOLIO (PAGE 2)

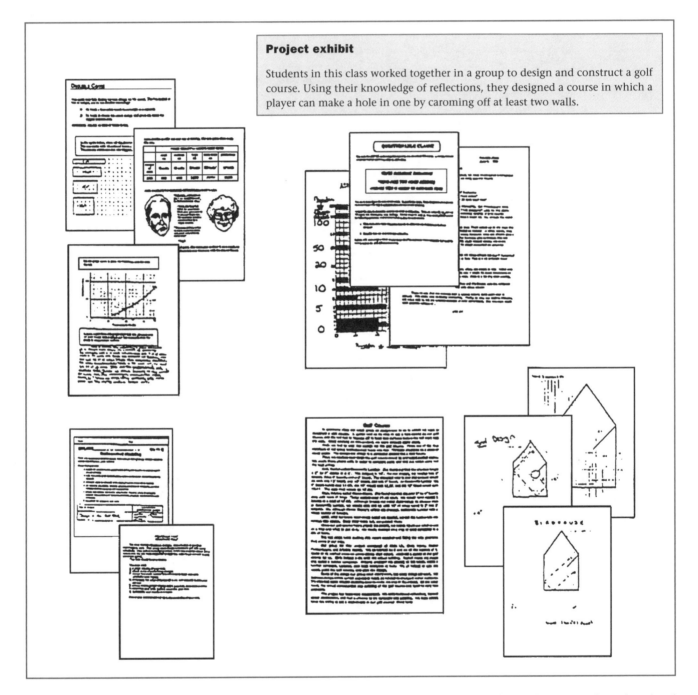

Project exhibit

Students in this class worked together in a group to design and construct a golf course. Using their knowledge of reflections, they designed a course in which a player can make a hole in one by caroming off at least two walls.

Reprinted with permission from New Standards™. The New Standards™ assessment system includes performance standards with performance descriptions, student work samples and commentaries, on-demand examinations, and a portfolio system. For more information contact the National Center on Education and the Economy, 202-783-3668 or www.ncee.org.

CHAPTER *2*

Collections of Work

FIG. 2.42

NEW STANDARDS™ PORTFOLIO (PAGE 3)

Problem-solving exhibit

Students must include four problems from their own work for this exhibit. Here is one of the four problems this student selected for this exhibit.

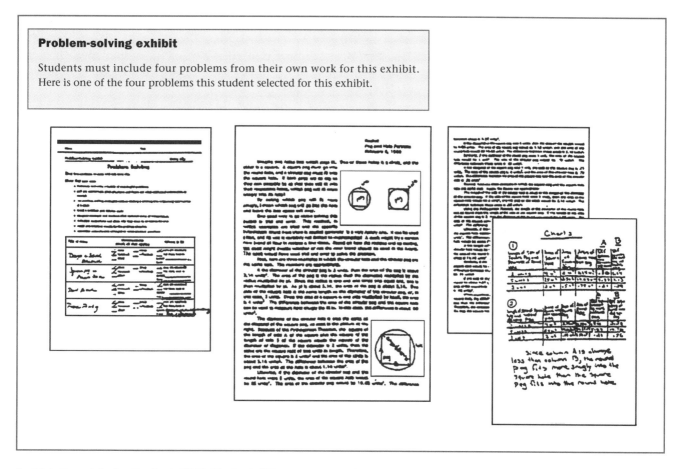

The New Standards portfolio is just one kind of portfolio—other kinds are organized on principles other than "exhibits" or "best work." Some may be organized around ideas of "showing growth over time," "work in progress," or content areas like number sense, geometry, or statistics.

Finding Good Assessment Tasks

READ ABOUT...

■ *For more reading about designing tasks, read "Assessing Students' Ability to Analyze Data: Reaching Beyond Computation" by Frances Curcio and Alice F. Artz (1996).*

■ *Twenty exemplary tasks for middle school students can be found in* **Exemplary Mathematics Assessment Tasks for the Middle Grades** *at the end of this book.*

WHAT DO I NEED TO THINK ABOUT IN GATHERING TASKS?

As we collect assessment tasks, we choose to use them "as is" or to adapt them. We have found the following questions helpful in thinking about whether the tasks are useful:

■ **What am I trying to find out?** How well do students understand the concepts? How well do students perform and understand the skills? How well will students use what they learn to solve problems? Can students explain what they know?

■ **Why is it important?** Is the concept or skill important in a wide variety of mathematical situations? Do students need to understand the concept in order to learn a new topic? Is it a skill students will frequently be asked to use? Is it an important strategy for solving problems?

■ **What are my criteria for success?** Is a correct answer sufficient? Do I expect students to provide more than one correct answer? Do I want students to justify their responses? Do I want students to use a skill or concept in a different situation?

■ **How will I use the evidence I get?** Will I make mid-course adjustments? Will I let students know the results? Do I want to know more about my students' thinking? Will I use it to determine a grade? Will I share the results with parents?

Good assessment tasks provide a positive instructional experience for students. We can use some of the same principles for gathering assessment tasks that we use for finding good instructional tasks. Some sources for good mathematics assessment tasks for middle-grades students appear in the following list.

Balanced Assessment for the Mathematics Curriculum. Purchase assessment packages from Cuisenaire-Dale Seymour Publications, P. O. Box 5026, White Plains, NY 10602-5026.

California Department of Education. *A Sampler of Mathematics Assessment*. Sacramento, Calif.: California Department of Education, 1994.

Kentucky Department of Education. Released open-ended tasks and performance events for grades 5, 8, and 12. For purchasing tasks, go to website www.kde.state.ky.us, then "Curriculum and Testing," then "News, Videos, Publications, and Teleconferencing."

Mathematical Sciences Education Board. *Measuring Up: Prototypes for Mathematics Assessment*. Washington, D.C.: National Academy Press, 1993.

Mathematics Department, Pittsburgh Public Schools, Connelly Learning Center, 1501 Bedford Ave., Pittsburgh, PA 15219.

New Standards Project. Contact National Center on Education and the Economy at website www.ncee.org.

Developing Assessments from Scratch

HOW DO I DEVELOP NEW ASSESSMENT TASKS FROM SCRATCH?

Sometimes we cannot find a task that assesses what we want. Developing assessment tasks from scratch can be fascinating and instructive for us and our students. Here are some general tips for constructing assessment tasks.

- **Avoid ambiguity.** Ambiguity in instructional tasks allows students to make different assumptions and use inappropriate approaches. Such ambiguity sometimes detracts from an assessment task. It is important that students know what we want them to accomplish and how they will be judged. A good assessment task makes sense and conveys purpose, even to students who do not perform well on the task.

- **Make the purpose clear at the beginning.** In instructional tasks, we sometimes ask students to do separate guided activities that are then brought together into a coherent whole. However, on assessment tasks, the students should clearly know the purpose of each task at the beginning, either explicitly through a simple checklist or implicitly by clearly worded questions.

- **Avoid choosing a context merely to provide interest.** Situations that add interest in instruction may distract in assessment. The context should make the problem easier, not harder. Try to avoid complicated contexts that are not directly related to the mathematics or contexts that are "gimmicks" intended only to provide interest.

- **Do not try to assess understanding of several concepts at once.** Longer tasks can be rich, allowing students to employ a variety of concepts and processes. Long tasks that cover too many different concepts may not provide accurate evidence of student understanding.

- **Avoid unnecessary cleverness in prompts.** Often a very straightforward prompt elicits the most creative work from students. A rule of thumb is that the task designer should write fewer words than he or she expects to get in the students' response.

Developing Assessments from Scratch

Below are guidelines for designing good assessment tasks developed by teachers in the New Standard Project.

1. Use language, context, and audience that are accessible and familiar to students:

- *Provide a context that does not require specialized knowledge.*

- *Keep language as simple and free of jargon as possible.*

- *Include tasks with visual clues (pictures or diagrams) and words to clarify.*

2. Provide students with an audience and a role to play within the problem situation:

- *Set the standard for mathematical communication.*

- *Make the purpose of the task apparent to students in a realistic way.*

- *Tap into students' interests.*

- *Give students opportunities to make decisions or express points of view that can be supported with mathematical reasoning.*

3. Create a task that has an authentic relationship to its context:

- *Use "real life" situations that allow for realistic reasoning.*

- *Find tasks that promote the use of a variety of mathematical models, tools, and resources.*

4. Make tasks accessible but well differentiated:

- *Find tasks that give all students a chance to enter the task and show positive achievement.*

- *Find tasks that are not limiting to less mathematically sophisticated students.*

- *Find tasks that give all students opportunities to think and reason about important mathematical ideas.*

5. Do not provide too much structure:

- *Find a balance between "structure" and "openness" (overstructuring can fragment tasks and providing too much guidance can limit the students' opportunities to think for themselves).*

- *Choose a mathematically rich situation that helps students make connections using essential mathematics.*

- *Provide an easy example (thus "using up" the trivial response).*

- *Show an incorrect method and ask students to state why it's incorrect.*

- *Include a response to a different task requiring the same type of product.*

CHAPTER 2

Developing Assessments from Scratch

How we develop a task depends on our needs and style. Listed below we offer two scenarios for how we might develop a new task.

SCENARIO 1: FROM DATA TO THE MATHEMATICS TO A TASK

An idea for a task begins with intriguing data or an intriguing situation, possibly found in the newspaper or a magazine. Questions might arise, "Where's the mathematics in this data or this situation?" or "What question or questions elicits this mathematics?"

Example: You read the headline: "No Record for 9.97 in the 99.96 Meter Race" in the sports section. It begs such questions as "Can you infer what might have happened?" (No record in the 100 meter race because the track was too short.) "How short?" (4 cm); What would the time have been if the track was the correct length? (9.97 seconds, using proportions?) A possible task might be to write a letter to the editor expressing your concerns about withdrawing the record.

SCENARIO 2: FROM THE MATHEMATICS TO A CONTEXT FOR THE MATHEMATICS

An idea for a task begins with a piece of important mathematics. The task grows out of answers to the question "Where would one find this mathematics or need to use this mathematics?"

Example: The mathematics of converting between fractions and decimals leads to the food store deli counter where you order 1 3/4 pounds of American cheese. The clerk slices the cheese, puts it on the scale, and stops when the scale reads 1.34 pounds. A possible task might be "Write what you would explain to the clerk to be sure you get the correct amount."

Developing Assessments from Scratch

TIPS FROM TEACHERS

■ *Start small and with low risk. Begin with one or two short open-ended questions, rather than a weeklong investigation question.*

■ *When you have an idea in November for an assessment question that will work best with what your class will be doing in February, sketch it out "then" so you remember it and return to it "later."*

■ *Write a short exam that focuses on a few important concepts before you teach the concepts. Then purposely prepare your students to pass the exam. This allows you to focus clearly at the outset on exactly what you want students to know and be able to do.*

■ *Include in the assessment task itself what sort of accomplishment earns credit for the students.*

■ *Before using an assessment question with students, give it to the teacher next door, your sixth grader at home, or anyone you can find. Ask whether the question is clear. Find out whether the reader knows what to do. Ask what he or she thinks the important mathematics in the problem is.*

A TASK DEVELOPMENT TEMPLATE

Bonnie Hole of the California Department of Education illustrates another way to think about developing tasks:

1. **Begin with an idea.**

2. **Test it.**
   Is it important or contextualized?

3. **Fashion it into a prompt.**
   What evidence of understanding or what processes does it elicit?

4. **Embellish it.**
   Can it yield more than one product or more than one kind of student work?

5. **Try it with students.**
   Do students see the mathematical purpose you see? Does the task elicit what they know?

6. **Revise it in light of students' responses.**

Interesting data found in encyclopedias, almanacs, sports record books, newspapers, and scientific databases can be used to create challenging tasks for middle school students. To increase your success rate when developing assessments from scratch, consider the suggestions for creating assessment questions listed in the"Tips from Teachers" column on the left-hand side of this page.

CHAPTER *2*

Expanding Tasks

HOW CAN I EXPAND TASKS THAT I HAVE FOUND?

We often find instructional tasks or closed-assessment tasks that are interesting or match the content we plan to teach, but they do not meet our assessment needs. For this reason, we must expand a task to make it work. **Figure 2.43** illustrates how a short task designed for individuals can be expanded into both a longer task and a group project.

FIG. 2.43

EXPANDING A TASK

> **A 15-minute task:**
>
> You receive the following request from the sixth grade at a nearby middle school.
>
> Dear Friends:
>
> Each year our school elects 25 representatives to the Student Council. In the past, they elected eight people from the sixth and seventh grades and nine from the eighth grade. That way, every class got the same number of people, except for eighth grade, which elected the president of the Council along with eight other representatives.
>
> This year we have 412 sixth graders, 336 seventh graders, and 252 eighth graders. We think that the sixth grade should get more representatives because our class is bigger than the others. Our ideas are just as good as the older kids' ideas. We should get our fair share of voices on the Student Council. Our problem is that we are not sure how to figure out exactly how many representatives to request and how to make our case to the student body.
>
> Please analyze our situation and help us decide how many representatives out of the 25 total each class should get so that we get our fair share.
>
> **Expanded to a one hour task:**
>
> Please submit your suggestions in a letter that we will duplicate and distribute to our student body to try to gain their support for changing how the Student Council is elected. Your letter should explain how to decide the number of representatives for each class and why your procedure is fairer than the present method. It is vital that you explain your proposal in a way that we can understand and apply in the future, even if the enrollments change. Your letter should also use graphics and any other devices that you think are appropriate to communicate your ideas as effectively as possible. It should be brief and well organized to succeed in making our point.
>
> **Expanded into a group project:**
>
> Finally, please be prepared to present your recommendations in a five-minute speech at our school assembly next week. You may want to bring posters or other visual aids to help your presentation.
>
> We really appreciate your helping us get better for our class on the Student Council. Thanks a million.
>
> Sincerely,
> Marion Middle School

READ ABOUT...

■ *For more information about expanding assessment tasks, read "Polishing a Data Task: Seeing Better Assessment" by Judith Zawojewski (1996).*

Chapter 3

Implementing an Assessment System: How Do I Put It All Together?

Teacher-to-Teacher

I have been learning as much about assessment as I can. I have gathered some very interesting open-ended tasks, and I am learning about portfolios and projects. Now, I need to know what to do with this stuff. I know that there is more to assessment than just giving my seventh-grade students good tasks. I need a system. How do I prepare my seventh graders for the new assessment? How do I manage my time? How do I set up my system for success? How do I ensure that my students do quality work? How do I help them perform up to my high expectations? I need to know how to put it all together.

READ ABOUT...

■ *Read about a seventh-grade teacher's struggle with her role during assessment in "To Help or Not" in* Mathematics Assessment: Cases and Discussion Questions for Grades 6–12 *(Bush 2000).*

Teacher Roles during Assessment

I start with the premise that all children are constantly trying to make sense of the mathematics problems they encounter. So if I can communicate well, I will understand the bases for their misconceptions. I ask questions that make them question their beliefs, create some disequilibrium and force them to think through the concept. My goal is to uncover what the students know to be true and the assumptions they are making. I find myself asking my students more and more "Does this always work?" "Under what circumstances does this not work?" "Can you find an example where this doesn't work?"

—Mary Bennion, seventh-grade teacher

WHAT IS MY ROLE DURING ASSESSMENT?

Our students' work during day-to-day teaching provides us with a wealth of information about their mathematical abilities. When we blend assessment into our daily lessons, we have many opportunities to understand how our students think mathematically.

The roles we take during assessment are multifaceted. Depending on our purpose for assessing, we can take on several roles as students work on an activity. **Figure 3.1** offers four different roles to consider. The illustrations in **Figures 3.2**, **3.3**, **3.4**, and **3.5** describe some of the things we do when we assume each role.

FIG. 3.1

TEACHER'S ASSESSMENT ROLES

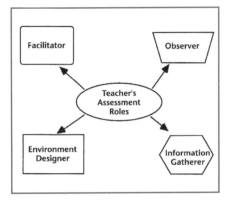

FIG. 3.2

ILLUSTRATION OF FACILITATOR ROLE

As a facilitator, you—

■ formulate focus questions that help students think through the problem and start to solve it;

■ pose questions to have students think about related problems they have previously solved;

■ have students think about alternative solutions or strategies;

■ clarify the task for students;

■ communicate standards;

■ ask nonjudgmental questions;

■ encourage collaboration with other students;

■ ask students to reflect on their thinking.

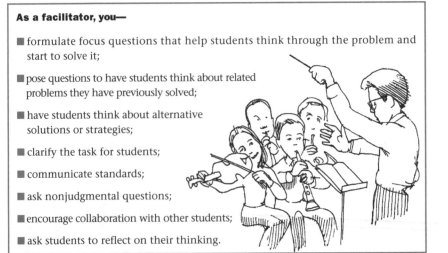

Teacher Roles during Assessment

FIG. 3.3

ILLUSTRATION OF GATHERER ROLE

As an information gatherer, you—

- observe students at work;
- listen to students talk with other students and with you;
- probe students' thinking;
- take notes;
- analyze student work at the moment and over time;
- seek background information about students.

FIG. 3.4

ILLUSTRATION OF OBSERVER ROLE

As an observer, you—

- walk around the room closely observing students' thinking and actions;
- use a variety of observation tools to observe for specific purposes;
- make mental or written notes about your observations;
- pull up a chair and watch students;
- observe how students start solving problems, where they get stuck, how they get unstuck;
- may let students know ahead of time what you are observing.

FIG. 3.5

ILLUSTRATION OF DESIGNER ROLE

As designer of the assessment environment, you—

- decide to group students or have them work individually;
- decide what materials and tools you will make available;
- create an environment in which students feel safe to experiment and inquire about mathematics.

Chapter Overview

In this chapter you will learn about—

- **teacher roles during assessment;**
- **creating a classroom environment conducive to effective assessment;**
- **managing time for assessment;**
- **conducting effective observations and interviews;**
- **promoting quality work from students;**
- **prompting students and revising students' work;**
- **assessing group work;**
- **promoting students' reflection and self-assessment.**

READ ABOUT...

■ *Read about the roles of teachers during assessment in* Mathematics Assessment: Myths, Models, Good Questions, and Practical Suggestions *and* Assessment Alternatives in Mathematics: An Overview of Assessment Techniques That Promote Learning *both edited by Jean Stenmark (1991, 1989). See examples of these assessment roles in* A Collection of Math Lessons from Grades 6 through 8 *by Marilyn Burns and Cathy McLaughlin (1996) and the videos entitled "Fraction Tracks" and "Building Rafts with Rods" in the Assessment Library by WGBH (1998).*

Establishing Conditions for Success

SOMETHING TO THINK ABOUT

What barriers keep all students from succeeding? How can these barriers be removed?

READ ABOUT...

■ *Read more about establishing conditions for success in* Measuring What Counts: A Conceptual Guide for Mathematics Assessment *by the Mathematical Sciences Education Board (1993) and* Student-Centered Classroom Assessment *by Richard Stiggins (1994).*

HOW CAN I USE ASSESSMENT TO ESTABLISH CONDITIONS FOR SUCCESS?

Decisions about the conditions that we set for assessment determine the kinds of evidence we get. These decisions also affect the quality of work our students produce. When we make decisions about assessing students, it is important to consider the conditions under which the students will work. See what students have to say about setting up conditions for success.

These students offer helpful suggestions about being fair with assessment. It is important that our students are given the best opportunity to show what they know and can do.

A STUDENT'S COMMENTS ABOUT MATERIALS

Having the right materials available during assessment is real helpful. If we get to use stuff in class, we ought to get to use it when we are being assessed. Sometimes it's just good to have things like rulers, calculators, or manipulatives available in case I need them. They help me think about the problems. Don't always give me what I need. Sometimes it's important to know which tool to choose.

A STUDENT'S COMMENTS ABOUT GROUP WORK

Sometimes being assessed in groups is helpful. Sometimes it's good to be assessed by myself. If we spend a lot of time in class working in groups, then we should get to work in groups when being assessed. Anyway, I always learn a lot working in groups. But at times I want the teacher to know what I can do by myself. I had a teacher once that did both—we worked awhile in groups, then we separated and gave our own answer. I liked that.

A STUDENT'S COMMENTS ABOUT TIME

I am usually a pretty slow worker. Sometimes I need time to think about problems, especially the hard ones. If I am given plenty of time, my work will be better. Sometimes I like to be able to finish a problem at home. This is especially true at the beginning of the year when we are getting back into the swing of things.

A STUDENT'S COMMENTS ABOUT HOMEWORK

I like to have some time in class to work on my homework so that I can get feedback. I also like to work a few problems together with other students in class. It is important that I understand the homework before leaving class. Sometimes I have spent a lot time working on the wrong assignment or working it a wrong way. I had a teacher once that required my parents to work some problems with me. I liked that.

Providing Equal Access

HOW CAN I ENSURE EQUAL ACCESS TO MY ASSESSMENT FOR ALL MY STUDENTS?

As teachers, it is important that we be alert to how the conditions or design of assessment activities may affect our students' performance. Some students may be at a disadvantage before the assessment even starts.

Listed below are some questions to consider as we create or select assessment tasks for our students:

- Do the tasks contain certain wording or vocabulary that may be unfamiliar to students?

- Are the contexts of the tasks familiar to students regardless of cultural or socioeconomic background or gender?

- Do the tasks make sense to students and are they motivating to students?

- Do the tasks include diagrams or pictures that make them clearer and more inviting?

- Do the tasks require information not accessible to all students?

In the right-hand column is advice from teachers who have had success in removing barriers for students.

POSSIBLY INACCESSIBLE TASKS

The following are two tasks that may be inaccessible to some students.

> You are traveling with your parents and in charge of gathering money for toll booths. The charge at the first toll booth is 55 cents. How many different ways can you make 55 cents using pennies, nickels, dimes, and quarters?

This task might be inaccessible to some students because some students, especially students living in rural areas, might not know what a toll booth is.

> A refrigerator costs $499 and the sales tax is 6 percent. It is on sale at 25 percent off. How much will the refrigerator cost your parents?

This task might be inaccessible to some students because it is not particularly motivating to most middle school students. Most students at this age are not interested or able to buy refrigerators, let alone figure the sale price.

READ ABOUT...

- *Read more about ensuring assessment accessibility in "Developing Communications Skills in Mathematics for Students with Limited English Proficiency" by Gilbert Cuevas (1991), in "Making Mathematics Accessible to Latino Students: Rethinking Instructional Practice" by Lena Khisty (1997), and in "Assessment and Equity" by Terri Belcher, Grace Coates, Jose Franco, and Karen Mayfield-Ingram (1997).*

TIPS FROM TEACHERS

- *Check the design of an activity or task before giving it to students. If necessary, revise it.*

- *Discuss unfamiliar vocabulary with students, or simplify the wording of a task.*

- *Ask students about the context of the task to see if they are familiar with it.*

- *Make sure students understand what the task is asking. If not, clarify it by adding questions that point them in the right direction without giving away the solution strategies.*

- *Ask students to paraphrase the task in their own words.*

Helping Weak Readers

READ ABOUT...

■ *Read more about helping students with weak reading skills in* Children Reading Mathematics, *edited by Hilary Shuard and Andrew Rothery (1984), and "Reading and Writing in Mathematics" by Mollie MacGregor (1993).*

WHAT CAN I DO TO HELP STUDENTS WHO HAVE WEAK READING SKILLS?

Students with weak reading skills are at a real disadvantage in mathematics assessment activities that require some reading. As we assess these students, we can use or alter tasks to make reading easier and to allow them to show us their mathematical capabilities. It is important that we create a safe environment that encourages students to ask questions and builds self-confidence. A variety of approaches can be used to help students understand the problem and show their solutions.

The list below contains some specific strategies that have been useful to teachers in helping weak readers:

■ Read the task out loud in class or have students read it in small groups.

■ Record the task on an audiotape. Poor readers can listen to it as many times as necessary.

■ Discuss the meaning of the question. Have the students rephrase it in their own words.

■ Clarify difficult vocabulary in a problem.

■ Encourage students to talk about the task. Sometimes students who feel embarrassed about not understanding the task may welcome the opportunity to ask questions.

■ Translate the task into the primary language of the student or pair students with others whose language is the same and have them translate it. (Pair-Share)

■ Use many representations, such as manipulatives, pictures, or charts, to explain the task.

■ Encourage students to give oral answers. Some students may have stronger verbal skills than writing skills.

■ Permit answers in different representations, such as diagrams or demonstrations with manipulatives.

■ Use and discuss a vocabulary list of mathematical terms. Keep the list posted in the room and add to it. Give students practice with difficult mathematical terms.

CHAPTER *3*

Helping Weak Readers

The activity in **figure 3.6** was designed by an ESL teacher to reinforce his students' mathematical vocabulary.

FIG. 3.6

STUDENT WORK—VOCABULARY PRACTICE

Mr. Meyers
Math – Room 317

Vocabulary Practice (A-K)

circumference	gallon	fraction	cone	greater than
average	kilometer	diameter	cylinder	hexagon
area	inside	horizontal	columns	common factor
corner	height	base	decimal	common multiple
angle	diagonal	denominator	grid	double

1. The bottom part of a _____fraction_____ is the _____denominator_____.

2. Square and rectangles have four _____angle_____.

3. To find the _____area_____ of a rectangle, you multiply the _____height_____ times the _____base_____.

4. A _____diagonal_____ is the line that runs from the top of a square on one side to the bottom of the other side.

5. Do you like your ice cream in a cup or in a _____cone_____?

6. A stop sign has eight sides so it is an octagon but a _____hexagon_____ has six sides.

7. You will find my basketball in the _____corner_____ of the room.

8. A can of beans looks like a _____cylinder_____.

9. I can run 6 _____kilometer_____ in about 20 minutes.

10. Martin must have been very thirsty because he just drank a _____gallon_____ of water.

11. 2, 3, and 6 are all _____common factor_____ of both 12 and 18.

12. A _____grid_____ has lines on it, like a calendar.

13. The _____average_____ score on the test was 87.4.

14. The numbers 98.4, 60.02 and 554.29 have _____decimal_____ but 67, 110 and 223 do not.

15. 60 and 80 are _____common multiple_____ of 2 and 5.

16. If you _____double_____ 167, you will get 334.

17. The area tells you how much space there is _____inside_____ a shape.

18. The _____circumference_____ tells you how far it is around a circle.

19. This room has 5 rows and 6 _____column_____ of desks.

20. Everyone knows that 617,834,209 is _____greater than_____ 37.

21. When you are on top of a mountain, the edge of the earth looks like a _____horizontal_____ line.

22. The line running through the center of a circle is the _____diameter_____.

Conducting Observations

Observing my students definitely added to my assessment of what they were accomplishing. My anecdotal notes proved far more revealing than merely the scores on their written work. If Nicholas were judged only by his writing, his masterful problem-solving abilities would not be acknowledged or understood. If I had just used a scoring rubric, I would have missed his ingenious sorting of structures. Although Thomas writes well, his high score on the written explanation would have shadowed some weaknesses he had with solving the problem at first. I would not have had any clue as to where Thao got stuck or why. Observation allowed me to see the failings of her initial strategy, her gaps in the way she ordered, and her logical thinking need more experience.

—Paula Ogri

HOW CAN I MORE EFFECTIVELY OBSERVE STUDENTS AT WORK?

Observing students while they work on tasks or activities gives us different information and a deeper understanding of our students' abilities. It allows us to closely watch the strategies that students use to get answers. Focused observations, rather than trying to observe all student performance at once, is a real time saver. Choosing the focus depends on what we want to learn about our students. For example, we might use the following questions adapted from *Mathematics Assessment: Myths, Models, Good Questions, and Practical Suggestions* (Stenmark 1991)to focus our observations:

- How does the student understand, define, formulate or explain the task?

- How does the student organize his or her approach to the task? What recording or tools, such as diagrams, graphs, or calculators, does he or she use?

- Does the student see relationships that may be present? Does he or she relate the task to similar problems done previously?

- Does the student vary the approach if one approach is not working?

- Does the student persist?

- Can the student describe strategies he or she is using? Does he or she articulate thought processes?

- Does the student show evidence of conjecturing, thinking ahead, or checking back?

- Does the student generalize about results or prove an answer?

- Does the student evaluate his or her own process, actions, and progress?

- How does the student work in the group?

- Does the student generalize about results or prove an answer?

CHAPTER *3*

Conducting Observations

Observing whole classes can be overwhelming. Consider the tips to the right from experienced teachers to get started.

FIG. 3.7

OBSERVATION GUIDELINES

OBSERVATION GUIDELINES
Middle School

Task Type	Grouping	Name
(open, closed, investigation)	(ind., pairs, group)	
_____	_____	_____

Task Description: _____

1. How does the student get started on the problem?
- A) Asks another student
- B) Asks teacher
- C) Self starts
- D) Does nothing
- E) Other/Comments: _____

2. When does the student get stuck?
- A) At the onset of the task?
- B) Sometime after having started the task
- C) When presenting (complete) solution
- D) Other/Comments: _____

3. What does the student do to get unstuck?
- A) Asks other students
- B) Asks teacher
- C) Copies another student
- D) Gives up
- E) Other/Comments: _____

4. What kinds of questions does the student ask?
- A) Rudimentary (How do I do it?)
- B) Clarifying (Is this what you mean?)
- C) Higher order
- D) Does not ask
- E) Other/Comments: _____

5. How does the student react to prompts?
- A) Becomes frustrated
- B) Ignores prompt
- C) Uses prompt successfully
- D) Uses prompt unsuccessfully
- E) Other/Comments: _____

6. What skills does the student demonstrate?
- A) Math skills (specifically, _____)
- B) Problem solving (specifically, _____)
- C) Reasoning
- D) Communication
- E) Other/Comments: _____

Conducting Observations

WHAT OTHER CLASSROOM ACTIVITIES MIGHT I OBSERVE?

What we observe depends on our focus. The observation forms in **figures 3.8** and **3.9** focus on different classroom activities. How are these forms alike and different? What is the focus of each?

FIG. 3.8

OBSERVATION FORM #2

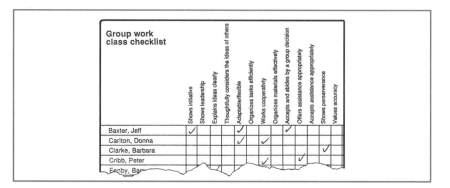

From Clarke, Doug, and Linda Wilson, "Valuing What We See." *Mathematics Teacher* 87 (October 1994): 543.

FIG. 3.9

OBSERVATION FORM #3

TABLE 1		
Activity	Group Participation	Listening Skills
Moves Orderly	Uses Quiet Voice	Uses Positive Support
Plans Group Action	Stays on Task	Overall Evaluation
	Oral Presentation	

	Student	Individual or Group Comments
TEAM 1	T*	
	E	
	A	
	M	
TEAM 2	T*	
	E	
	A	
	M	
TEAM 3	T*	
	E	
	A	
	M	

(+) Indicates a strong performance in a skill area calling for special mention during group presentation.

(−) Indicates a deficient performance in a skill area calling for discussion during group presentation or evaluation.

If no + or − is present in a behavioral category, the student's performance is considered satisfactory in that category.

*T = Recorder, E = Encourager, A = Artist, M = Materials Manager.

From Baxter, Stephen, and Teresa Lasley, "Valuing What We See." *Mathematics Teacher* 85 (November 1992): 638.

CHAPTER *3*

Conducting Observations

HOW DO I DESIGN MY OWN CHECKLIST?

Sometimes it is useful to design our own observation checklist. In **figure 3.10** is a generic observation checklist developed by Doug Clarke and Linda Wilson that allows us to focus on any category we wish.

FIG. 3.10

BLANK OBSERVATION CHART

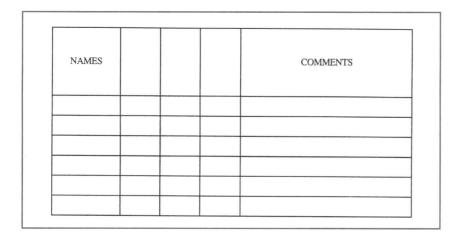

In this checklist, we may choose two or three categories on which to focus. Possible categories for the columns in our self-designed checklist might include—

- shares ideas;

- asks questions;

- encourages peers;

- looks for different approaches.

We can then write group members' names in the left-hand column and put a mark beside each observed example as it happens. Finally, we may write comments that are useful for documenting in the last column.

READ ABOUT...

- *Read more about effective observation in* Assessment Alternatives in Mathematics *by David Clarke (1988),* "Valuing What We See" *by Doug Clarke and Linda Wilson (1994), and* Mathematics Assessment: Myths, Models, Good Questions, and Practical Suggestions, *edited by Jean Stenmark (1991).*

Conducting Effective Interviews

HOW CAN I EFFECTIVELY INTERVIEW STUDENTS?

TIPS FROM TEACHERS

■ *Scatter interviews over the course of the whole term in order to interview each student individually at least once.*

■ *Interview students in small groups.*

■ *Conduct interviews when the rest of the class is engaged in an independent activity.*

Another way to assess students' thinking is through interviews. Such interviews may take many forms and can be designed for different purposes. The information we gather from interviews provides insight into students' understanding and thinking that might be missed through observations or examination of work. Through interviews, we can learn more about students' mathematical strengths and weaknesses. Interviews are also excellent tools for uncovering mathematical misconceptions because they help us track their origins.

Student interviews can be formal. That is, we create specific questions in advance, pose them to students, and record the responses on a recording sheet or on audiotape or video. Interviews can also be informal and extemporaneous. That is, we may begin asking students questions based on their response to a task or question or from something noticed during an observation. Asking students a few questions when we circulate around the room or dismiss students at the end of the period may be considered an interview.

A common challenge with interviewing is finding the time to do it. Some teachers have found ways to interview their students regularly. Interviews can be conducted in a variety of situations. We may interview students about their responses to a problem of the week or to an open-ended question. Interviews may also focus on larger pieces of work such as a portfolios or investigations. We may choose to ask questions about how students used manipulatives, calculators, or other tools or why they set up a chart or drew a diagram a certain way.

Interview questions should be nonjudgmental and designed to detect the student's train of thought. Some generic questions you can ask about any problem follow:

■ When you began to solve the problem, what were you thinking?

■ Why did you choose to solve the problem that way?

■ Can you show your solution in another form?

■ How would the answer be affected if the numbers were bigger or you did not have this information?

■ What was it about the numbers that led you to reason this way about them?

■ How did you know to...?

■ Does it make a difference that...?

■ Is one of these answers better or are they both as good?

CHAPTER *3*

Conducting Effective Interviews

REVEALING STUDENT THINKING

We may decide not to interview all of our students but to focus instead only on particular students, perhaps because their work is unclear, exhibits some problem, or is exemplary. After scoring a piece of a student's work, we may wish to pursue why the student responded in a certain way.

For example, **figure 3.11** illustrates a response to a task from an ESL student.

FIG. 3.11

STUDENT WORK—RESPONSE FROM AN ESL STUDENT

Diagonally Speaking
(Adapted from Marilyn Burns)

Investigate the number of diagonals in different polygons. Tell how many diagonals are in polygons that have 3, 4, 5, 6, 10, 15, and 35 sides. Look for patterns. Try to write a rule for a polygons with n sides. Be sure to explain your process and reasoning carefully.

side	diagonals
3	0
4	2
5	5
6	9
10	35
15	90
35	560

If you have 100 sides of polygon. How many diagonals have in 100 sides.

frist you use 100 − 2 = 98 and than use 2 + 98 = 100. form 2 to 98 have how many pair and use how many pair to time 100. and the you find out the answer that is how many diagonals. have in 100 sides.

$100 \times 48.5 = 4850$ diagonals.

After scoring his work, the teacher wanted more information about this student's thinking. Here are some questions she posed to the student:

- Why did you decide to solve the problem of how many diagonals there would be in a 100-sided polygon?

- Why did you think 100 − 2? Where did the 2 come from?

- How did you figure out that you should think about pairs?

- How does thinking about pairs help you to figure out the rule?

Conducting Effective Interviews

READ ABOUT...

■ *Read about how a student's thinking is revealed when a fifth-grade teacher interviews his students in "When the Wrong Way Works" in* Mathematics Assessment: Cases and Discussion Questions for Grades K–5 *(Bush 2001)*

SOMETHING TO THINK ABOUT

Some teachers have students interview each other. What are the advantages and disadvantages of this strategy?

Asking questions that are related directly to the mathematics of the task will reveal more about the student's thinking. Some teachers use a tape recorder or take notes to document an interview. Others have found it is difficult to juggle writing and thinking about what to ask next and simply make mental notes.

Figure 3.12 provides an example of an interview conducted by a middle school teacher. Note the questions asked of the student.

FIG. 3.12

SAMPLE INTERVIEW BETWEEN TEACHER AND STUDENT

I roved and observed. They were motivated to beat their measures and excited when they did. In my wanderings, I happened to glance at Hugh's recording sheet. I was intrigued. He had recorded his giant step as 130 29/31 cm. I needed to talk to Hugh.

Me: Hugh, how's it going?

Hugh: Good! I'm going to beat my giant step. I know it. Wanna watch?

Me: Sure. How long was your last one?

Hugh: *(Referring to his record)* $130\frac{29}{31}$ cm.

Me: *(Pointing to the fraction)* Tell me about this here. What does it mean?

Hugh: Well I almost jumped 131 cm, so I wrote it that way. It means I was really close.

I still needed to know more. It wasn't a fraction that I expected to see, but Hugh was impatient. Everything seemed obvious to him and he wanted to get on with breaking his record. I decided to leave him to it and returned to the conversation later when the activity was over.

Me: You know Hugh, I've been thinking about what you told me about your jumping. I'd like you to explain why you chose $\frac{29}{31}$

Hugh: I just did. *(Long pause)* You know, you can choose anything you want.

Me: What if you had chosen 78?

Hugh: Well, then I wouldn't have 29, I'd have 72. No, probably 74.

Me: And if you had chosen 15?

Hugh: Probably 13 or 14 ... 'cause it was close to the next one.

Me: The next one?

Hugh: *(Sounding impatient with me)* Yeah, to 131.

I still needed to talk, and I could tell that Hugh was ready for the conversation to end. I decided to introduce another model and hope he would stick it out so that I could probe a bit more. A perfect question popped into mind.

Me: So you say that the number can be anything. I understand. Here's a straw and I'm putting my thumb against it. What if I decide that the straw is 20. How long would you say my thumb is?

Hugh: *(Taking a look)* Well, your thumb isn't 15. So it's 5. Yeah, $\frac{5}{20}$.

I still couldn't let go. I was more and more intrigued and distracted by Hugh's thinking.

Me: You say that the straw can be anything, and I think I understand. But I'm wondering, can it be anything? Is there a number that wouldn't work to describe the length of my thumb?

Hugh: *(Responding in a flash)* It couldn't be a third ... no, not a third. 'Cause it's smaller ... No, I couldn't use thirds. *(A long pause—for some reason which I didn't question. I could see he was still thinking about it. A huge smile appeared across his face)* Oh wait! I could do it in thirds. It's about as long as $\frac{3}{4}$ of a $\frac{1}{3}$ of the straw. *(A short pause)* So I can use thirds.

From Barnett, Carne, Dona Goldstein, and Babette Jackson. *Fractions, Decimals, Ratios, and Percent: Hard to Teach and Hard to Learn?* Portsmouth, NH: Heinemann. (pp. 52–53). Reprinted with permission from Heinemann, copyright © 1994.

CHAPTER 3

Managing Time

HOW CAN I BEST MANAGE TIME?

At the outset, finding time to assess is often the greatest concern and problem. How do I find the class time to give open-ended tasks and have students perform them? How do I find time outside class to score work from five classes? How do I find the time to let students revise their work? How do I find the time to manage portfolios? When can I observe or interview students? Time for these assessment strategies often competes with our need to "cover the curriculum." The valuable evidence we gather and the knowledge students gain through quality assessment are so powerful we must seek ways to solve the time problem.

The best source for tips about saving time comes from teachers who have implemented successful assessment programs. Here are some of their strategies for making more effective use of valuable time.

TIPS FOR SAVING TIME

■ *Begin using a variety of assessments over a period of time rather than all at once. Use one tool or strategy at a time and wait until students reach a reasonable level of comfort with it before moving on to another tool or strategy.*

■ *Stagger work from different classes. Give open-ended tasks to only one class at time.*

■ *Grade sample tasks, not all of them.*

■ *Have students select their "best" items, such as their best journal entry for the week, to turn in.*

■ *Ask students to make a checklist of all the task requirements and have them check off what they have finished.*

■ *Use a "comment" sheet that lists the most common errors or omissions. Check off the ones that apply to the students' work you are grading.*

■ *Use a lot of classroom observation as well as correction of papers.*

■ *Have students work in groups and take turns submitting assignments. Instead of having 32 papers to score per class, you have 8 if groups of 4 are used.*

■ *Use peer assessment and self-assessment. Ask students to read and evaluate one another's work.*

■ *When scoring students' work, use only two levels such as "acceptable" or "unacceptable."*

READ ABOUT...

■ *Read about a group of teachers in a mathematics department struggling with the issue of finding time for portfolio assessment in "I Just Collected 120 Portfolios—Now What?" in* Mathematics Assessment: Cases and Discussion Questions for Grades 6–12 *(Bush 2000).*

SOMETHING TO THINK ABOUT

How does time, or lack of it, affect assessment decisions? What would you do differently if time were not a factor?

Promoting Quality Work

TIPS FROM TEACHERS

■ *Lead class discussions and brainstorm about what good mathematics work should include. Keep the brainstormed list posted. The list below was developed by a seventh-grade ESL class:*

1. The answer has to be accurate and reasonable.

2. The writing shows details so that someone who is not in the class can understand it.

3. There are complete sentences. The writing isn't necessarily long.

4. The person uses examples.

5. The person has a lot of ideas about the problem.

6. There is more than just one answer.

7. The paper should be clean.

8. The person followed all the directions.

I presented the area problem to students. I then reviewed a general rubric with them and discussed what each level and score meant. I held up a blank piece of paper and asked students to imagine that it was their completed solution to the area problem. I told them to envision that the paper had received a "4" on our rubric. Students then discussed what the paper would look like, and we made a list of these characteristics on chart paper. While the students were working on the problem, I continually referred them to the "Quality Work List." I eventually collected the work and looked over their solutions. Unfortunately, this was a very difficult problem to solve independently, especially the explanation part for my second-language learners. I selected two examples to share with the students so that we could discuss them before they revised their work. In retrospect, I think I should have used an easier task to get them used to this process.

—Susan Killebrew

HOW CAN I PROMOTE QUALITY WORK IN MATHEMATICS FROM MY STUDENTS?

When assessing students, we would like to see their best performance on tasks. Communicating to them our requirements for quality work in mathematics is one way to accomplish this. This strategy will let them see precisely the kind of work we would like them to produce. The "Tips from Teachers" columns on this page and the next contain some strategies collected from teachers who have successfully promoted quality work from their students.

CHAPTER *3*

Promoting Quality Work

Figure 3.13 provides a sample of quality student work.

FIG. 3.13

SAMPLE OF A STUDENT'S QUALITY WORK

Problem Statement

This problem is about a family of five and I am part of the family. The problem wants us to tell weather their our brother, sister, mom, grandmother, and etc. The problem said that the average of the families age is 23 year, so the problem wants me to find out what are each of their ages.

Process

First I multiplied 5×23=115 years because there are 5 people in the family and the average age is 23 and I multiplied it to get the total of the unknown ages. Then I wrote down the people who are in my family inclid me. Next to the word me, I put down age 12 because that's my real age. Then I subtracted 12–115=103 to get the left over age. Next to the word dad I wrote 40 which means he's 40 years old. Then I subtracted 103–40=63 ye. to get the years left over. For my mom I decided that she should be 36 years old. Then I subtract 63–36=27 years left. Then I wanted my brother to be older than me so I wrote down 14 next to the word brother which ment that he is 14 years old. Then I subtracted 27–14=13 years left. I had only 13 years left and one more family member, so I just put 13 next to the word sister, so my sister is 13 years old.

After all that I added up all the ages and the answer was 115. Then I divided 115 by 5 and got the average of 23.

They are related to me because their my mom dad, brother, and sister.

Solution

I know my answer is right because when I divided 115 by 5 it equaled the average of 23 and the problem said that the average is 23.

Evaluation

I think this problem was easy because I did these problems a lot of times before, so I understand the problem and know what to do.

TIPS FROM TEACHERS

■ *Share student work that represents good mathematics work. Remove students' names to make it anonymous. On occasion, borrow work from another class or teacher. Ask the class to anlayze what makes the work strong. For example, in the student's work in **figure 3.13**, we might point out that the student clearly communicated her reasoning and solution.*

READ ABOUT...

■ *Read about a teacher's strategy to have her students develop their own rubric in "Students as Assessors" in* Mathematics Assessment: Cases and Discussion Questions for Grades K–5 *(Bush 2001).*

SOMETHING TO THINK ABOUT

Some teachers believe that sharing expectations with students will "Let the cat out of the bag." That is, students will learn what to do through the expectations. What do you think about this practice?

Promoting Quality Work

MORE TIPS FROM TEACHERS

■ *Ask students to choose good examples of work that meet each criteria for a specific task. Discuss the work with the students.*

■ *Break up a task into smaller parts and discuss the parts.*

■ *Have students create a rubric about what good work should contain. (See chapter 4 for a definition of a rubric.) Have the class add to the rubric as the year progresses and as they get better with assessment. The following rubric was developed by an eighth-grade class:*

4 *Accurate answer*
  Has a lot of ideas about the problem
  Includes details
  More than one answer or way of getting answer

3 *Close to perfect answer but missed something*
  Not as much detail as a **4**

2 *Does not have the right answer but has an idea of what he or she is doing*
  Left things out or didn't finish

1 *Didn't follow directions*
  Answer not complete
  Needs improvement in explaining

■ *Have students look at work from each grade level below and above around the same type or topic of the task.*

■ *Keep good work samples from previous years or different classes to show to students.*

■ *Use an easy task and have students create papers of fictitious students with a score of 1, 2, 3, and 4 each. The fictitious papers in* **figure 3.14** *were created by eighth-grade students in Kentucky.*

CHAPTER *3*

Promoting Quality Work

FIG. 3.14

STUDENT SAMPLE OF FICTITIOUS 4, 3, 2, 1 WORK

Today your teacher put this figure on the chalkboard and asked the students to copy it into their math journals.

Your friend, Raul, is sick today. After school you decide to call him and describe the figure so that he can draw it in his math journal.

In your student response booklet, write how you would describe the figure to Raul over the phone.

Sample responses:

4	If I had to describe the figure to Raul over the phone, I would tell him to draw a circle. Then, I would tell him to draw a rectangle but that half of it is inside the circle on the circle's left side. Next I would tell him to draw a triangle directly centered on top of the rectangle but that the right corner of the triangle would be inside the circle. Last I would tell him to erase any lines of the circle that are inside another shape.

3	First make a medium triangle so that the point is facing up. Draw a rectangle under the triangle so that the rectangle is on its side and touching the triangle. Then draw a large circle to the right halfway in the rectangle and about an inch in the triangle. Erase the line going through the triangle and rectangle.

2	There's a big circle behind all of the shapes. There's a small triangle on the curve close to the top. There's a long rectangle right under the triangle. The rectangle is halfway in front of the circle.

1	First you will make a big circle, and next you will make a rectangle, and last you will make a triangle. And then you will have your thing done in your journal.

1992–93 KIRIS Common Open-Response Item. Reprinted with permission from the Kentucky Department of Education. Note that KIRIS has been replaced by the Commonwealth Accountability Testing System.

Promoting Quality Writing

I start by having students explain the meaning of a problem orally to a partner in their own words. Each student takes a turn restating the problem. The pairs use these sentence starters:

> *This problem is about _____.*

> *This problem wants us to find out _____.*

Writing together to produce one problem statement, the pair can then construct a paragraph that precisely describes the problem by clearly restating it. Alternatively, the class can construct a whole-class statement by having the teacher take suggestions for each sentence, deciding together how to clarify the sentence, and having the teacher record the final sentences on butcher paper.

The next step gives students practice describing the process they went through to solve the problem. To the whole class, a student talks through each step he or she took in the process of solving the problem. The teacher records each step on the overhead, modeling how to write the process clearly and accurately. Different students talk through their steps to the class and have their solution process recorded by the teacher. In this way, the teacher creates models of "process" writing. Different models are posted around the room and kept on the wall during the semester.

Once students have seen different models of written work through the process above, they work in pairs or groups of four to write together to produce one "process" description. They address these questions to help them sequence and describe their thinking: What did you do first? What strategies did you use? Why did you do what you did? What did not work? Why? What did you do next?

—Delia Levine

Promoting Quality Writing

HOW CAN I FOSTER HIGHER QUALITY WRITING IN MY STUDENTS?

Students need regular opportunities to write about their mathematical thinking to become better writers and better thinkers. One good writing task is to have students explain strategies and solutions using words, mathematical symbols, graphs, diagrams, or other representations. Here is an example of writing instructions that promote communicating about mathematical thinking (from *They're Counting on Us*, California Mathematics Council [1995]).

Your math writing assignment has two parts. First, you are to restate the problem in your own words. Then you are to show your solution. Remember, you are to show all your work as well as your final answer. Be sure to—

1. Write your solution as if the reader knows nothing about the problem.

2. Show all your math work, including all calculations.

3. Organize your work into either a step-by-step plan and solution or some kind of chart or table that is easy to read and follow.

4. Proofread your work so you are sure you have not left out any important words or calculations.

5. Make sure this is your best work. Make sure it is neat and legible.

Promoting Quality Writing

Getting our students to write about mathematics is often challenging. As with any skill, the more experiences students have, the greater their proficiency will become. Writing about mathematics is an ability that can be taught. Below are suggestions from teachers to help develop better student writing:

■ I try to improve my students' writing about mathematics by breaking down the writing process into several components and teaching it through a step-by-step process. I write comments on their work and have them work in groups to revise it. Below is an example of a process description written by my sixth graders along with my comments. I intentionally used a task that was easy for my students in order to allow them to focus on writing about their thinking. The problem I gave to my students was the following:

I have some three-legged stools and some four-legged chairs. If I have exactly 29 legs of furniture, how many stools and how many chairs do I have?

(**Fig. 3.15** provides a sample of a student's work on this task.)

FIG. 3.15

STUDENT WORK—FURNITURE PROBLEM

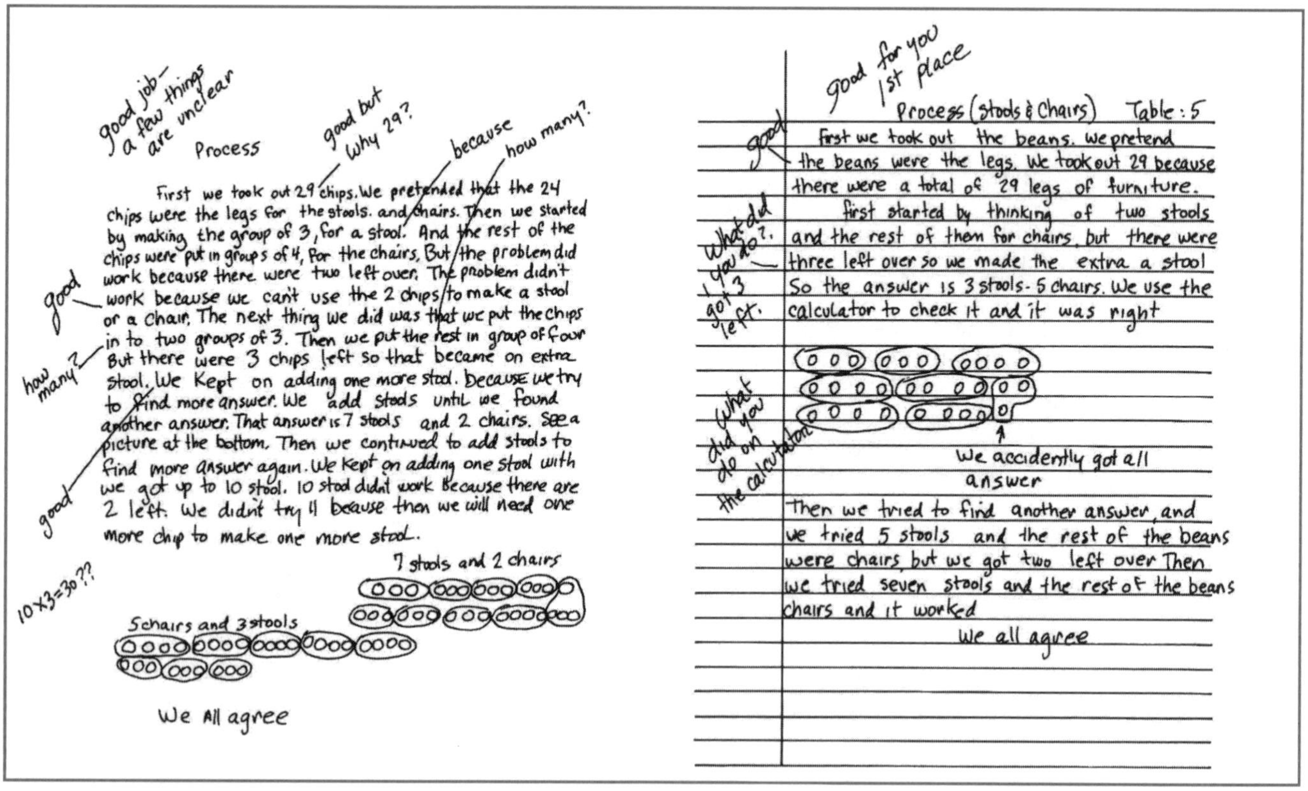

Promoting Quality Writing

■ I have students write to a variety of audiences, such as a younger child, a best friend, the principal, a parent or caregiver, or the president of a company.

■ I have students write directions that involve a sequence of ideas. For example, I might ask students to write about going from my classroom to the school office. I check the writing by having other students follow the instructions and suggest revisions.

■ I offer written comments on students' first drafts or have other students give suggestions about how to clarify the writing. Below is an example of the guide my students use.

> Do all your math work on a separate sheet of paper. Include all of your work, even strategies that did not work. Work until you have exhausted all the possibilities.
>
> Write the process paragraph. In your paragraph, you need to explain how you solved or tried to solve the problem. Connect what you are doing to the clues in the problem. Even if you did not find a solution, write that process in your paragraph. Remember, successful problem solvers look for other solutions or explain mathematically why only one solution exists.
>
> Next, write a short solution paragraph. This paragraph must prove your answer is correct. Convince someone that your answer is correct but do not retell the process. Make sure to refer to the clues in the problem. Please don't tell me it is the right answer because you checked it or it fits all the clues.

READ ABOUT...

■ *For more about promoting quality writing, read "The Missing Link? Writing in Mathematics Class!" by John Ciochine and Grace Polivka (1997); "Exploring Middle Graders' Mathematical Thinking through Journals" by Mary Lou DiPillo, Robert Sovchik, and Barbara Moss (1997); "No Time for Writing in Your Class?" by Margaret McIntosh (1991); and "Journal Writing: An Insight Into Students' Understanding" by Karen Norwood and Glenda Carter (1994).*

Prompting Students during Assessment

WHEN SHOULD I PROMPT STUDENTS AND HOW MUCH PROMPTING IS REASONABLE?

Prompting students while they solve a mathematics task can be tricky. On the one hand, we do not want them to get discouraged or frustrated. On the other hand, we want to see their work, not ours.

Thinking ahead of time about some of the difficulties our students might have with the task will help some, especially if we create some questions that will promote thinking without giving away the solution strategies. It generally comes down to using our best professional judgment to guide the amount of prompting we do and the type of prompts we give. Generally, when students have less experience solving open-ended or complex tasks at the beginning of the year, it is usually best to offer more prompts. As students gain experience solving these types of tasks, less prompting may be required.

In any case, we should avoid prompts that "give away" strategies or solutions to the task. Below is an example of an open-ended task with possible prompts:

■ *What numbers from 1 through 36 can be written as the sum of consecutive whole numbers?*

■ *Which numbers cannot be written as the sum of consecutive whole numbers?*

■ *What patterns do you notice and why do you think they occur?*

Figure 3.16 provides an example of student work on this task.

FIG. 3.16

STUDENT WORK—CONSECUTIVE WHOLE NUMBERS TASK

Sum	2 addends	3 addends	4 addends	5 addends	6 addends	7 addends
1						
2						
3	1+2					
4						
5	2+3					
6		1+2+3				
7	3+4					
8						
9	4+5	2+3+4				
10			1+2+3+4			
11	5+6					
12		3+4+5				
13	6+7					
14			2+3+4+5			
15	7+8	4+5		1+2+3+4+5		
16						
17	8+9					
18		5+6+7	3+4+5+6			
19	9+10					
20				2+3+4+5+6		
21	10+11	6+7+8			1+2+3+4+5+6	
22			4+5+6+7			
23	11+12					

Sum	2 addends	3 addends	4 addends	5 addends	6 addends	7 addends
24		7+8+9				
25	12+13	12		3+4+5+6+7		
26			5+6+7+8			
27	13+14	8+9+10			2+3+4+5+6+7	
28						1+2+3+4+5+6+7
29	14+15					
30		9+10+11	6+7+8+9	4+5+6+7+8		
31	15+16					
32						
33	16+17	10+11+12			3+4+5+6+7+8	
34			7+8+9+10			
35	17+18			5+6+7+8+9		2+3+4+5+6+7+8
36		11+12+13	(also 8 addends: 1+2+3+4+5+6+7+8)			

11x MR0092 (March 27, 199C) © Balanced Assessment   A Sampson Solution

CHAPTER 3

Prompting Students during Assessment

Prompts that may be given to this student might include the following:

- *What does "consecutive" mean?*

- *What is an example of a number that can be written as a sum of consecutive whole numbers? What are the addends?*

- *Can 3 be written as the sum of consecutive whole numbers? How?*

- *The number 15 can be written as the sum of consecutive whole numbers in exactly three different ways:*

    $$15 = 7 + 8$$

    $$15 = 1 + 2 + 3 + 4 + 5$$

    $$15 = 4 + 5 + 6$$

- *What are some other numbers that can be written as the sum of consecutive whole numbers?*

- *What numbers have two or more consecutive addends?*

- *How can you organize your solutions so you see the patterns easily?*

- *What patterns do you notice?*

When asking students to look for patterns, offering the following prompts might be too leading because they give away an important idea about the pattern:

- *Which of these numbers are prime numbers?*

- *What do you notice about the consecutive sums of prime numbers?*

Some open-ended tasks often require students to interpret the task first by stating their assumptions. With these tasks, our prompts should help students clarify the task and their assumptions on their own, rather than our providing the assumptions for the task. Below is an example of a task in which students must make some assumptions.

A locally-owned car wash advertises that they have millions of satisfied customers each year. Is this claim sensible? (From Glencoe *Interactive Mathematics*)

Some questions generated by students tackling this problem might include:

1. *How many hours will the car wash be open?*

2. *How long does it take to wash a car?*

3. *How many cars can the car wash clean at once?*

4. *Where is the car wash—in a populated part of town or in a rural area?*

Prompting Students during Assessment

Some students may need more prompts than other students. An effective way to respond to the students' need for more guidance is to answer each of their questions with a question. Read the dialogue of a teacher who is prompting a student having difficulty with a problem in **figure 3.17**.

FIG. 3.17

PROMPTING DIALOGUE (FROM NCTM *ASSESSMENT STANDARDS* [1995])

Inside, Out, and All About

Janna McKnight perched on the edge of her desk at the back of the classroom. Her sixth grade students were elbowing each other and chatting while parading to the front of the room to place their yellow stickies on a bar chart. They had been finding the area of a salt marsh on a map, a rather irregular shape. Each stickie represented the area (in thousands of square meters) determined by one student.

Mathematics Standard: Encouraging students to make conjectures and seek verification involves them in doing significant mathematics.

The portion of the chart from about 85 to 95 was beginning to look like the New York City skyline, with high-rise towers huddled close together. Close in, to the left' and right of the city, were several lower towers. Off to the right at 196 was one lonely stickie with the initials TP, and down to the left were two other stickies at 55 with the initials BT and AK.

Ms. McKnight called the class to order. "All right, let's see what you've found. Who'd like to make some observations about our data?"

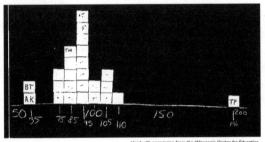

Used with permission from the Wisconsin Center for Education Research. School of Education University of Wisconsin—Madison

"Ninety-two thousand square meters got the most, but 87 was a close second," Jeremy answered. "It seems like lots of people got answers between 86 and 94."

"The lowest answer was 55—two people got that—and the highest was 196. Those people must have done it wrong, because those answers are, like, too different to be true," Angel offered.

Students should make connections between area and perimeter in meaningful contexts instead of learning those topics as isolated, formula-based skills.

"Bernice, is the 55 with BT on it yours?" Wallace blurted.

"The 196 is mine, and it isn't wrong!" Tyler offered in a defensive tone.

Anthony interrupted. "Bernice and I worked together, but I think our calculator gave us the wrong answer. I just added it up again, and ours should be 85 instead of 55."

Equity Standard: Perceptive questioning helps all students explain what they know and can do.

"Tyler, would you like to explain how you found 196 as the area of the marsh?"

"Well, you remember how we put string around those circles the other day? You didn't give us any string today. But my sweatshirt has a string in the hood, so I pulled it out and wrapped it around the marsh. Then I straightened it out into a square on top of the plastic, and it was about 14 units long and 14 wide. So its area was about 196. The square wasn't exactly 14, but it was pretty close!"

"So, Tyler found the area of a square he built from reshaping a string that fit around the perimeter of the marsh. I noticed most of the rest of you doing something quite different. Amy?"

Amy explained that her group had put clear plastic graph paper on top of the marsh and counted squares. Dyanne explained how her group counted partial squares as halves or fourths for more accuracy.

"Did anyone approach the problem differently? What do you think about Tyler's procedure?"

"I think it's a lot better," said Richard, "because Tyler didn't have to do all that counting. I wish I'd thought of making it into an easier shape. It would have saved a lot of work."

"But why is Tyler's answer so much bigger?" asked Nancy. "I don't know why it's wrong, but Tyler's answer is way too big."

"If the distance around the marsh is a lot, then the area is a lot—wouldn't that be right? Like when one is big, the other is big?" asked Cindy. Numerous heads nodded in agreement, amid a few dissenting frowns.

Pointing to the bulletin board, where dot-paper records of a geoboard activity from the previous week were displayed, Dyanne reminded the class that shapes with equal perimeters could have very different areas.

"All right," said Ms. McKnight, glancing at the clock over the chalkboard. "We're not going to have time today to get to the bottom of this mystery. Let's just write Tyler's conjecture on the board and see whether we can investigate it further tomorrow. Who can use some good mathematical language to say what Tyler's been thinking?"

CHAPTER 3

Prompting Students during Assessment

MORE PROMPTING STRATEGIES

Another prompting strategy is simply to respond to students with general questions that require them to reflect on their work or the problem. Some general prompting questions might include:

- *Look back at the problem. What is the task asking you to do? Restate the problem in your own words. What are all the things your answer needs to address to be complete?*

- *What problem does this one remind you of?*

- *What mathematics do you know that might be useful in this problem?*

- *What is the one thing you can try to get started on this problem?*

A final strategy for prompting is to have students work in small groups or with partners. Often many questions can be answered by peers. The main problem with this strategy, however, is that other students tend to help by giving answers rather than hints. We will need to prepare our students to give good prompts.

READ ABOUT...

- *For more about prompting students, read* Teaching Problem Solving: What, Why and How *by Randall Charles and Frank Lester (1987).*

- *Read about a seventh-grade teacher's concerns about prompting students as they tackle an open-ended task in "Open Car Wash" in* Mathematics Assessment: Cases and Discussion Questions for Grades 6–12 *(Bush 2000).*

SOMETHING TO THINK ABOUT

How do you feel about having your students prompt each other? What are the strengths and weaknesses of this practice? How might you prepare them to provide valuable assistance to other students without giving away the solutions?

Revising Student Work

TIPS FROM TEACHERS

■ *Have students work in small groups or with partners. They trade papers and try to follow one another's solutions. They can ask one other questions to clarify their explanations. For example, if a student writes, "I added the number," another student might ask, "Which numbers did you add?" or "Why did you add those numbers?"*

■ *Select papers that show a range of response levels. Type the answers or cover up the names to make the responses anonymous. Ask students to score the papers by using a given rubric. Then discuss how to make the papers better.*

■ *Ask one of the classes to assess another class's work and write comments for revision.*

■ *Give students a task to solve. Then show them a rubric. Let students go back and revise their responses according to the rubric.*

SOMETHING TO THINK ABOUT

Some teachers believe that using correct mathematics vocabulary is an important requirement for good writing in mathematics. Others feel that mathematics thinking is most important. How do you feel about this difference of opinion? What weight should correct vocabulary carry in assessing mathematics writing?

I adapted the strategy suggested by Marilyn Burns in her lesson on "Introducing Algebra" from A Collection of Math Lessons from Grades 6 to 8, *which emphasizes the importance of clear and specific writing in mathematics. Students were asked to figure out how many squares are on the border of a 10×10 grid. From this concrete example, students generated six possible methods to find the answer. Each student wrote a description of the method that made the most sense to him/her.*

I typed up some examples, and the next day, I put them on the board and showed the students how a few minor changes in wording helped clarify explanations. Together as a class we practiced with several other examples. Then I gave them a handout with five written explanations that needed revision. Each student wrote a revision on scratch paper. Then, working in pairs, they discussed their revisions and together came up with one final revision. The discussions were great and the quality of writing improved tremendously.

—Mary Bennion

HOW MUCH REVISION OF STUDENT WORK SHOULD I ALLOW?

Revising involves "revisiting" students' work to improve its quality. The process is important in order to help students further reflect on their work and the work of their peers. It communicates to students that good work requires time and revision. It also provides a clear way for us to communicate our expectations. We can help students develop self-monitoring strategies by having them think about their first attempts at solving problems and then consider how they might improve their responses.

Although providing quality revisions is time-intensive, most teachers who do it believe the time is well spent. All revising, however, need not fully fall on the teacher. After being initially "shown" how to improve their papers, students can eventually take more responsibility. Moreover, offering students concrete reasons for revising is important. They must believe that revision is not simply busy work. Some reasons for quality revisions might include publishing a class or school newsletter, making a presentation to peers or parents, or developing a portfolio entry.

The number of revisions we allow students is our decision. Some teachers believe students should revise as many times as they like. Others believe that students should revise once. As students gain experience with the revision process, they begin to incorporate strategies into their initial responses that they used previously in revisions. Listed later in this section are some strategies used by teachers who have their students revise work often.

CHAPTER *3*

Revising Student Work

WHAT QUESTIONS SHOULD I ASK IN REVISING STUDENT WORK?

Some key questions we might ask students to help them revise include:

- What was the task asking?

- What would a clear explanation include?

- Would someone who was not in our class understand it?

- Are all the elements of the answer included?

- How can this response be more precise? Be more concise? Be clearer? Be more convincing?

Figure 3.18 provides some examples of revisions produced by two seventh-grade students. Working together, they revised descriptions of how to figure out how many squares are on the border of a 10×10 grid.

FIG. 3.18

STUDENT WORK—WRITTEN EXPRESSIONS OF MATHEMATICAL IDEAS

State which method is being described. Then each pair member writes an improved version on a separate sheet of paper. Share your revisions with your partner. Decide on the best revision and record it on this sheet.

1. There are four sides, and when you don't count the corners, you get 8 x 4 = 32, and you add the corners and get 36.

This is method #6. There are 10 squares on each side of the square. Since you can't count the corners more than once, you add all the cornerless sides first. With no corners, each side would have 8 squares. Then you add the 4 corners. 9+8+8+8+4=36

2. First you count how many cubes go down the left and right and then count the top and bottom cubes. Left and right have 10 and top and bottom 8. Now you add all the numbers and get 36.

This is method #5. First you count how many squares go down left and right, which is 10 squares. Then you count the top and bottom, leaving out the corners because they we already counted by the left and right. So on those

3. The perimeter is 36. You can figure this out by multiplying 9 and 4 because it is easier than doing any other method.

Think of each side as 9 squares, (leaving the corners out). Each side takes one corner to make it even btween the four groups. Now, each group has 9 squares. Multiply the amount of squares in each of the groups by 4 because there are 4

4. There is 10 on top, 9 on both sides, and 8 on the bottom = 36.

This is method #2. First you count the squares on top, which is 10 squares. The you count the ones on the left and right sides, which is 9 because you don't want to re-count the corners on top. And the bottom squares are the remaining 8 because both of its corners were

5. I knowthere are 10 on each side. So 10 + 10 + 10 + 10 = 40 squares but I have to subtract 4 because a square has 4 corners. 40 – 4 = 36

This is method #1. There are 10 squares on each side, so you add 10+10+10+10 or 10x4 (because there are 4 sides). In doing this each corner has been added one time too many. So you subtract the 4 extra times and get 36

② sides you would count 8 squares. Last you would add up the numbers you counted, 10+10+8+8

③ groups. That will give you the answer of 36.

④ already counted with the left & right sides.

Then you add up all of the sides. 10+9+9+8=36.

Promoting Student Reflection and Self-Assessment

HOW CAN I BETTER PROMOTE STUDENT REFLECTION AND SELF-ASSESSMENT?

It is important that our students reflect on their work and thinking processes. Self-assessment helps students view their accomplishments in light of their strengths and areas for improvement. As with other assessments, the tools we use to promote reflection and self-assessment are varied. When students are first asked to reflect on their work or assess themselves, their responses may be superficial. With experience and encouragement, however, their responses will deepen. Listed below are tools that other teachers have used to promote reflection.

Journals

Some teachers ask students to write regularly in journals. Students can do *free writing*, where they write about what they wish, or they may write to specific prompts that are given to them. The two-column journal described below is a popular strategy.

One approach to journal writing is to have students divide the journal into two columns. In the first column, they describe the mathematics activity they have completed. In the second column, they answer questions and write reflections. Here are a few examples of questions they can address:

■ How could you apply this problem at home or on a job?

■ How does this problem connect to another subject area or a real-life activity?

■ How does it connect to a previous activity we have done?

■ What part was the most challenging? Why?

CHAPTER 3

Promoting Student Reflection and Self-Assessment

Providing students clear criteria for writing in their journals will help them understand what is expected from them. Consider the following guidelines for students.

Please communicate freely and openly in your journal. Your teacher will review your journal periodically, looking for evidence of the following—

- communication (verbal and pictorial) of your mathematical thinking (you try to make clear and detailed explanations and diagrams)

- mathematical reasoning

- personally derived solutions to math problems

- creative insights and deep thinking (e.g., you make conjectures and generalization, etc.)

- monitoring and reporting your feelings (disequilibrium, AHA!s, joy, frustration, etc. that you experienced while working on a problem or during a class activity)

- awareness of your own mathematical growth, strengths, and needs

It is important not to erase a journal entry, even if you believe what you wrote before is wrong. Instead, show growth by adding new ideas (write the date that you make the addition). Or, on another page, describe how your thinking has changed.

Group Reflections

Teachers may also ask students to reflect on group work. After students have solved a problem in cooperative groups, ask them to reflect on the group process as well as their mathematical solution. The group can then write one group reflection piece together. Questions like "How did you all work together?" or "Describe the process your group went through to reach your solution" might provide interesting responses.

Promoting Student Reflection and Self-Assessment

Another strategy is to ask students to complete sentence starters like these from the Math Learning Center below:

As a group, I think we …

As a group member, I am pleased how I …

As a group member, I think I need to …

One or more positive thoughts I would like to share about each of my groupmates …

Self-Scoring of Work

Eventually students should be encouraged to score their own work using a criteria we give them or criteria they identify. Teachers may also want them to write a justification of the score they gave themselves.

In addition to self-assessment, peer assessment may be used. Teachers may ask other students to score their peers' work and justify their score. It is sometimes interesting to compare the self-scores and justifications with those given by other students.

Figure 3.19 provides an example of how a sixth-grade ESL student scored another students' work, along with her reasons for the score.

FIG. 3.19

STUDENT WORK—KELLY'S SCORE SHEET

Code	grade	reason	Group
F	4	well explanation, has a lot of ideas about the problem, complete sentence, follows directions, correct spelling, reasonable	4
D	3	not as much detail, almost got the answer but something is missing, no example	2
B	4	gives examples, reasonable, easy to understand	4
C	2	wrong spelling, no example not as neat, hard to understand, not reasonable, something is missing	2
A	2	something is missing, not reasonable can't understand, no example.	3
H	3	give example, not as much detail, something is missing	2

Promoting Student Reflection and Self-Assessment

Prompts

Teachers can use specific prompts during class or seatwork to promote student self-reflection. Below are some prompts that might be used.

- *How did you participate with your group this week?*

- *Explain how you worked a problem with your group.*

- *Student-led parent conferences are coming up. What do you think would be important to tell your parent about your work in math class?*

- *Choose one piece of work in your portfolio. Tell how you might improve it.*

- *If you could change something in mathematics class, what would you change? Be specific about one change and how it would look to you.*

- *Think of a teacher who has inspired you in mathematics. What did he or she do?*

- *Reflect on the scaling, ratio, and proportion activities we have been doing in class. Write about two ways you can use scale, ratio, and proportion in your daily life.*

Promoting Student Reflection and Self-Assessment

The "Thought Starters" below from the Math Learning Center can be used for any mathematical activity.

Today I felt my inner mathematician at work when …

Today I experienced the power of a model when …

Today I felt the importance of math as a social activity when …

Math is an ongoing process! Today I developed a better understanding … when …

I felt disequilibrium today when …

A mathematical idea that fascinated me today was …

Today I saw a connection between _____ and _____ when …

A math problem I'm working on (or wondering about) is …, and here is my reasoning so far …

I think …

I wonder …

AHA! …

What if …

A conjecture I have is …

A generalization I have is …, and here is how I decided …

A question I have is …

Here is where I became "stuck" today …

What happened to help me get "unstuck" was …

CHAPTER 3

Promoting Student Reflection and Self-Assessment

Reflection Activities

The Shell Centre for Mathematical Education (Bell, Crust, Shannon, and Swan, 1992) developed a handbook of reflection activities. These suggestions are taken from their handbook:

- Have students make up mathematical problems.

  1. Give students an answer to a problem and have them make up a corresponding question.

  2. Give students a collection of data and have them formulate questions.

  3. Have students make up questions about a particular situation, context, or topic. For example, create one easy and one hard problem about money.

- Present students with a finished piece of work containing errors. (You may create the work and use a fictious student name.) Ask students to score the work and correct errors. Have them write comments to the fictitious student explaining how to avoid the errors in the future. Ask students to think about the following questions while writing their comments:

  1. What advice will you give this student?

  2. How might this comment help him or her?

  3. Can you explain more fully where you think he or she may be going wrong?

Promoting Student Reflection and Self-Assessment

■ Have students interview each other in pairs about their work on a project, at the end of the unit, or on a portfolio piece. Use the interview checklist in **figure 3.20.** The interviewer makes notes on the interviewee's replies.

FIG. 3.20

INTERVIEW CHECKLIST

Interview Checklist

You will need a partner. Take turns asking each other these questions. Make notes of your answers.

1. What were you asked to do in this lesson?
Show me an example.

2. In what ways did you work?
Were you, for example ...
     listening to explanations?
     discussing?
     practicing skills you already had?
     solving problems?
     using practical equipment?
     experimenting and investigating?

3. What do you think you were expected to learn?
What did you learn?

4. What were the most important ideas?
Make a list of these.

5. What was the hardest thing about this topic?

6. How well did you understand the work?
Is there something that you still don't fully understand?

7. What mistakes did you make?
Why did you make these mistakes?

8. What choices did you make while you were working?
Why did you choose the way you did?

9. Why do you think your teacher gave you this work to do?

10. Do you have any tips for someone else who has to do this work?
What should they do first? How should they work?
What should they watch out for?

11. Are there any connections with the mathematics you have done before?
What mathematics did you need to know already in order to do this work?

12. Is there anything else you would like to say about this topic?

CHAPTER *3*

Promoting Student Reflection and Self-Assessment

■ Have students reflect on ways of working in mathematics class. Ask students to complete the "Math Metacognition Survey" in **figure 3.21**. Afterwards, have them debate the advantages and disadvantages of each of the statements.

FIG. 3.21

METACOGNITION SURVEY

Math Metacognition Survey

Metacognition means thinking about how you do something, so this Math Metacognition Survey is about what you think about doing mathematics. Please answer each question carefully by circling *True* if you agree with the statement or *False* if you disagree with the statement.

1. You learn more from working on one hard problem than from working on ten easy problems.	True	False
2. You learn more by listening to someone else explaining something than by trying to explain it yourself.	True	False
3. Working with a partner is better than working on your own.	True	False
4. You learn more by working on problems than by listening to an explanation, however good it is.	True	False
5. Copying work from the board or textbook is a very helpful way of learning.	True	False
6. When you are stuck, it's better to put your hand up and wait than to ask your neighbor for help.	True	False
7. Discussing mistakes is a waste of time; the teacher should just tell us how to get things right.	True	False
8. You can learn just as much from watching other people working on a problem as you can from doing it yourself.	True	False
9. You can learn a lot from trying to make up your own questions.	True	False
10. You learn more by working on a lot of short problems than by working on a few longer investigations.	True	False
11. You should never copy another person's work.	True	False
12. You learn more from getting things right than from getting things wrong.	True	False

READ ABOUT...

■ *For more about promoting reflection, read* Mathematics Assessment: Myths, Models, Good Questions, and Practical Suggestions, *edited by Jean Stenmark (1991) and "Student Self-Assessment in Mathematics" by Patricia Kenney and Edward Silver (1993).*

Chapter 4

Using the Results of Assessment: What Do I Do with the Work I Have Collected?

Teacher-to-Teacher

I have gathered lots of evidence about what my seventh-grade students know about and can do with mathematics. Now what do I do with it? Before, I took their scores from tests, quizzes, and homework and figured their grades. I simply computed the percentages and found averages. Now, however, I have observation and interview notes, writing samples, projects, tests, and quizzes. The evidence I have about each student is very different. How do I translate this work into a grade? Moreover, how do I let the students and parents know how well my students are doing? It is hard to compare students with the evidence I have gathered. I need some help making sense of all that I have gathered.

READ ABOUT...

■ *Read more about scoring and grading in "Scores and Grades: What are the Problems? What are the Alternatives?" by Judith Zawojewski and Richard Lesh (1996).*

Designing and Using Rubrics

WHAT IS THE DIFFERENCE BETWEEN SCORING AND GRADING?

We prefer to think about assessment as a tool to improve teaching and learning. Having selected or developed assessments and implemented them within a system, we face important decisions about using the evidence we have gathered. How do we effectively and efficiently score, interpret, report and make decisions on the basis of what we have learned about our students?

Throughout this book, we have defined *assessment* to mean the process of gathering evidence about what students know and are able to do. We now introduce the term *evaluation* to mean the process of making judgments, or placing "value," on the evidence. The two most common methods of making these judgments are *scoring* and *grading*. Scoring is comparing students' work to a *standard*. The standards are designed to communicate our expectations for students' work and provide us with a structure for reliably and accurately scoring that work. Scoring students' work then becomes an evaluation—when we place a value on a piece of evidence. Grading, conversely, is what we do with a set of scores to summarize or compare students' performance and communicate it to others.

In summary, students' work that is gathered through assessment is scored by means of standards. These scores can then be assigned grades. In this manner, value is placed on students' work, and it is evaluated.

WHAT IS A RUBRIC?

We are in the process of developing our second rubric for scoring problems that require students to justify their response. After talking with colleagues, I think I need to simplify my expectations and go back and start with a very simple problem, graduate to a "middle" level problem, and then present a complex problem. I should let the students compare and contrast work at each level and then have them develop a rubric that can be used with all levels of work.

For practical purposes, we will define *rubric* to mean a *hierarchy of standards used to score students' work*. Rubrics help us keep the focus of our assessment on performance rather than on the performer. We often use rubrics to assign scores to samples of students' work—most often on a four-, five-, or six-point scale.

Well-designed rubrics allow students to see descriptions of the requirements for their performance. Teachers who have used rubrics successfully report that their students produce higher quality work when they know the rubric used for scoring.

WHAT TYPES OF RUBRICS ARE AVAILABLE?

There are two basic types of rubrics: holistic and analytic. Holistic rubrics describe the qualities of performance for each performance level. The score students receive through holistic rubrics depends on what level of performance they have achieved. Students receive one numerical score, such as a 2 or a 4, for one task. By assigning *one* score to the work, we judge the work on its overall quality.

Holistic rubrics are usually general. That is, they may be used to score any mathematical task. One of the simplest generic rubrics that middle teachers have found useful is the following four-point scale:

1 Wow............Work is full and complete

2 Okay............Minor errors, but core understanding is evident

3 Hmmm.........Serious errors, but some understanding evident. Work must be redone

4 Yucky............Minimal effort and/or little or no evidence of understanding

Other general holistic rubrics, like the one in **figure 4.1** are more complex.

In this chapter you will learn about—

■ developing and using rubrics to score students' work;

■ strategies for scoring students' work;

■ converting scores to grades;

■ giving feedback to students;

■ making instructional decisions based on assessment evidence;

■ reporting assessment results to parents.

GRADES 6–8 ■

FIG. 4.1

HOLISTIC RUBRIC

GENERIC ON-DEMAND RUBRIC

"4," "5" Accomplishes the task.

The response accomplishes the prompted purpose. The student's strategy and execution are at a performance level consonant with the relevant standards cluster (skills, conceptual understanding, or problem solving and communication), and qualitative demands of the task. Even for tasks that are very open regarding content, the content chosen by the student must serve the purpose well. Communication is judged by its effectiveness, not by grammatical correctness or length.

Although a "4" need not be perfect, any defects must be minor and very likely to be repaired by the student's own editing, without benefit of a note from a reader.

Distinguished performances are nominated for "Distinguished Performance" recognition, the "5." A distinguished performance is exciting—a gem. It excels and merits nomination for distinction by meeting the standard for a "4" and demonstrating special insights or powerful generalizations or eloquence or other exceptional qualities. A score of "5" is not applicable for every task.

"3" Ready for needed revision.

Evidence in the response convinces you that the student can revise the work to a "4" with the help of written feedback. The student does not need a dialogue or additional teaching. Any overlooked issues, misleading assumptions, or errors in execution—to be addressed in the revision—do not subvert the scorer's confidence that the student's mathematical power is ample to accomplish the task.

"2" Partial success.

Part of the task is accomplished, but there is lack of evidence—or evidence of lack—in some areas needed to accomplish the whole task. It is not clear that the student is ready to revise the work without a conversation or more teaching.

"1" Engaged task with little success.

The response may have fragments of appropriate material from the curriculum and may show effort to accomplish the task, but with little or no success. The task may be misconceived, or the approach may be incoherent, or the response might lack any correct results. Nonetheless, it is evident that the respondent tackled the task and put some mathematical knowledge and tools to work.

0 No Response of off task

When the response is blank, it is scored an "NR" (no response). When there are marks, words, or drawings unrelated to the task, it is scored "OT" (off task). In either case, there is no evidence that the task was engaged.

Reprinted with permission from New Standards™. The New Standards™ assessment system includes performance standards with performance descriptions, student work samples and commentaries, on-demand examinations, and a portfolio system. For more information contact the National Center on Education and the Economy, 202-783-3668 or www.ncee.org.

Designing and Using Rubrics

Analytic rubrics, conversely, assign scores to the components of a task. We assign specific points for completion of each of these components and add these scores to obtain an overall score for the task. In **figures 4.2** and **4.3** are examples of analytic rubrics.

FIG. 4.2

ANALYTIC RUBRIC

MATHEMATICAL SKILLS	RATING
Calculation/estimation: compute with integers, decimals; use a calculator to compute with large numbers	**4**– proficient **3**– adequate **2**– marginal **1**– unsatisfactory

KEY MATHEMATICAL UNDERSTANDING	RATING
Measurement: estimate; make and use measurements to describe phenomena	**4**– thoroughly developed **3**– partially developed **2**– minimally developed **1**– not developed
Number: understand, represent, and use numbers in a variety of forms	**4**– thoroughly developed **3**– partially developed **2**– minimally developed **1**– not developed

CRITICAL PROCESS UNDERSTANDING	RATING
Reasoning: use concepts and operations logically, appropriately	**4**– thoroughly evident **3**– substantially evident **2**– partially evident **1**– minimally evident
Problem Solving: with a variety of representations that enhance understanding	**4**– exemplary **3**– effective **2**– marginal **1**– unsuccessful
Connections: implicitly or explicitly connect multiple representations; show threads of reasoning that tie the calculations to larger issues	**4**– substantially connected **3**– partially connected **3**– partially connected **2**– minimally connected **1**– not connected
Communication: convey findings and understandings	**4**– exemplary **3**– effective **2**– marginal **1**– unsuccessful

CHAPTER *4*

From the Connecticut Common Core of Learning Mathematics, Joan Baron, 1992. Reprinted with permission from the Connnecticut State Department of Education.

Designing and Using Rubrics

FIG. 4.3

ANALYTIC RUBRIC

READ ABOUT...

■ *Read about middle school teachers trying to develop a rubric in "A Room with More Than One View" by Jean Stenmark, Pam Beck, and Harold Asturias (1994).*

TABLE 1

ANALYTIC SCORING SCALE*

Understanding the problem	**0**: Complete misunderstanding of the problem
	3: Misunderstanding or misinterpreting part of the problem
	6: Complete understanding of the problem
Planning a solution	**0**: No attempt or totally inappropriate plan
	3: Partially correct plan based on part of the problem's being interpreted correctly
	6: Plan that leads or could have led to a correct solution if implemented properly
Getting an answer	**0**: No answer or wrong answer based on an inappropriate plan
	1: Copying error, computational error, or partial answer for a problem with multiple answers
	2: Incorrect answer following from an incorrect plan that was implemented properly
	3: Correct answer and correct label for the answer

*Adapted from Charles, Lester, and O'Daffer (1987, p. 30)

From Kroll, Diana Lambdin, Joanne Masingila, and Sue Tinsley Mau. "Grading Booperative Problem Solving." *Mathematics Teacher* 85 (November 1992): 623.

How are these rubrics alike or different? How do they compare with the holistic rubric on page 95. Which do you think is easier to use?

Designing and Using Rubrics

Interestingly, the mathematics portfolio assessment of the Kentucky state assessment system has recently shifted from a holistic scoring rubric to an analytic scoring rubric. **Figures 4.4** and **4.5** illustrate both rubrics. Look at them carefully to see how they differ. Which would you prefer to use?

The type of rubric we use is a matter of preference and need. Some of the advantages of using each type of rubric are listed below.

Advantages of Holistic Rubrics

■ Work judged by overall quality

■ All processes given equal weight

■ Thinking processes and mathematical communication stressed

Advantages of Analytic Rubrics

■ Stresses different steps in solving tasks

■ Some processes may receive more weight or emphasis

■ Allows for partial credit

■ Easier to apply

Designing and Using Rubrics

FIG. 4.4

KENTUCKY HOLISTIC SCORING RUBRIC

Kentucky Mathematics Portfolio HOLISTIC SCORING GUIDE 1994–95	An individual portfolio is likely to be characterized by some, but not all, of the descriptors for a particular level. Therefore, the overall score should be the level at which the appropriate descriptors for a portfolio are clustered.			
	NOVICE	**APPRENTICE**	**PROFICIENT**	**DISTINGUISHED**
PROBLEM SOLVING — Understanding/Strategies, Execution Extensions	■ indicates a basic understanding of problems and uses strategies ■ implements strategies with minor mathematical errors in the solution without observations or extensions	■ indicates an understanding of problems and selects appropriate strategies ■ accurately implements strategies with solutions, with some observations or extensions	■ indicates a broad understanding of problems with appropriate strategies ■ accurately and efficiently implements and analyzes strategies with correct solutions, with extensions	■ indicates a comprehensive understanding of problems with efficient, sophisticated strategies ■ accurately and effectively implements and evaluates sophisticated strategies and correct solutions and includes analysis, justifications, and extensions
REASONING	■ uses mathematical reasoning	■ uses appropriate mathematical reasoning	■ uses perceptive mathematical reasoning	■ uses perceptive, creative, and complex mathematical reasoning
MATHEMATICAL COMMUNICATION — Language, Representations	■ uses appropriate mathematical language some of the time ■ uses low mathematical representations	■ uses appropriate mathematical language ■ uses a variety of mathematical representations accurately and appropriately	■ uses process and appropriate mathematical language most of the time ■ uses a wide variety of mathematical representations accurately and appropriately; uses multiple representations within some entries	■ uses sophisticated, precise, and appropriate mathematical language throughout ■ uses a wide variety of mathematical representations accurately and appropriately; uses multiple representations within entries and states their connections
UNDERSTANDING/ CONNECTING CORE CONCEPTS	■ indicates a basic understanding of core concepts	■ indicates an understanding of core concepts with some connections	■ indicates a broad understanding of some core concepts with connections	■ indicates a comprehensive understanding of core concepts with connections throughout
TYPES AND TOOLS	■ indicates low types; uses low tools	■ includes a variety of types: uses tools appropriately	■ includes a variety of types: uses a wide variety of tools appropriately	■ includes all types; uses a wide variety of tools appropriately and thoroughly

Reprinted with permission from the Kentucky Department of Education. Please note that KIRIS is no longer the state assessment system in Kentucky. It has been replaced by the Comonwealth Accountability Testing System.

Designing and Using Rubrics

FIG. 4.5

KENTUCKY ANALYTIC SCORING RUBRIC

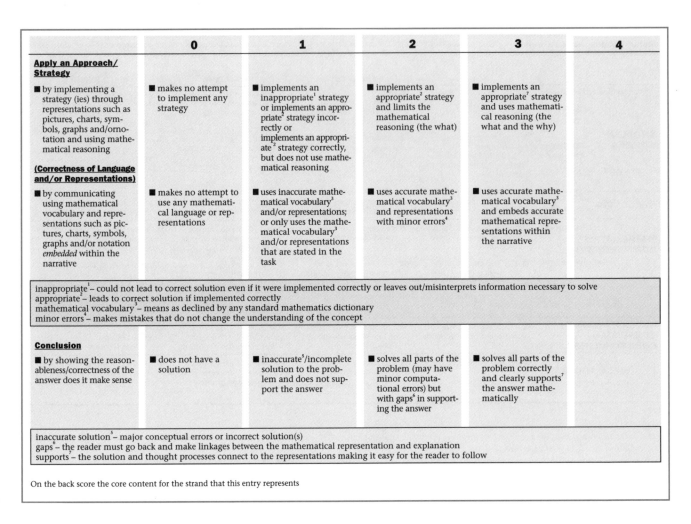

	0	**1**	**2**	**3**	**4**
Apply an Approach/ Strategy ■ by implementing a strategy (ies) through representations such as pictures, charts, symbols, graphs and/or notation and using mathematical reasoning	■ makes no attempt to implement any strategy	■ implements an inappropriate[1] strategy or implements an appropriate[2] strategy incorrectly or implements an appropriate[2] strategy correctly, but does not use mathematical reasoning	■ implements an appropriate[2] strategy and limits the mathematical reasoning (the what)	■ implements an appropriate[7] strategy and uses mathematical reasoning (the what and the why)	
(Correctness of Language and/or Representations) ■ by communicating using mathematical vocabulary and representations such as pictures, charts, symbols, graphs and/or notation *embedded* within the narrative	■ makes no attempt to use any mathematical language or representations	■ uses inaccurate mathematical vocabulary[3] and/or representations; or only uses the mathematical vocabulary[3] and/or representations that are stated in the task	■ uses accurate mathematical vocabulary[3] and representations with minor errors[4]	■ uses accurate mathematical vocabulary[3] and embeds accurate mathematical representations within the narrative	

inappropriate[1] – could not lead to correct solution even if it were implemented correctly or leaves out/misinterprets information necessary to solve
appropriate[2] – leads to correct solution if implemented correctly
mathematical vocabulary[3] – means as declined by any standard mathematics dictionary
minor errors[4] – makes mistakes that do not change the understanding of the concept

| **Conclusion**
■ by showing the reasonableness/correctness of the answer does it make sense | ■ does not have a solution | ■ inaccurate[5]/incomplete solution to the problem and does not support the answer | ■ solves all parts of the problem (may have minor computational errors) but with gaps[6] in supporting the answer | ■ solves all parts of the problem correctly and clearly supports[7] the answer mathematically | |

inaccurate solution[5] – major conceptual errors or incorrect solution(s)
gaps[6] – the reader must go back and make linkages between the mathematical representation and explanation
supports[7] – the solution and thought processes connect to the representations making it easy for the reader to follow

On the back score the core content for the strand that this entry represents

CHAPTER *4*

Designing and Using Rubrics

HOW DO I GET MY STUDENTS INVOLVED IN DESIGNING RUBRICS?

We may wish to involve our students in designing rubrics for certain tasks. Designing their own rubrics encourages students to think through expectations for quality work. Student-designed rubrics promote ownership of the assessment process because the expectations for work are stated in the students' own terms.

> *Show your work.*
>
> *Explain your thinking.*
>
> *Neat.*
>
> *Label your answer.*
>
> *Reader is able to understand our work.*
>
> *Solution makes sense.*
>
> *The math is right.*

The following are strategies for getting students to design their own rubrics:

■ *Before having students design their own rubrics, have them score papers with a rubric that the teacher developed.*

■ *Start with an easy task or one below grade level and give students good examples of each performance level as described by the rubric.*

■ *Start with a task that has one correct solution. Tasks with multisolutions are more difficult to construct rubrics for.*

■ *Have the students divide class papers into two piles, high and low. Then have them divide the work into four piles, each pile representing one of the four levels of the rubric. Ask students to think about the kind of mathematical thinking that each level contains.*

■ *Let students use a dictionary or thesaurus to help find words that convey degrees of proficiency.*

READ MORE ABOUT IT

■ *For more examples of rubrics, read* "A Teacher's Views on Classroom Assessment: What & How" by De Tonack (1996) *and* "Assessing Mathematical Processes: The English Experience" by Malcolm Swan (1996).

■ *Read how one teacher had students develop their own rubrics in* "Students as Assessors" in Mathematics Assessment: Cases and Discussion Questions for Grades K–5 *(Bush 2001).*

Scoring Student Work

HOW DO RUBRICS HELP ME SCORE AND ANALYZE STUDENT WORK?

Here is how one teacher used a simple rubric to analyze students' work:

I just concluded a unit on fractions, decimals, and percents with my sixth grade students using the Connected Mathematics Project unit "Bits and Pieces, Parts I and II." I decided to assess my students' understanding of the integration of these concepts using an adapted task from the Balanced Assessment Project—"Basketball or Baseball." (See figure 4.7 for a sample of solid student work on the task.)

This task focused on the students' ability to write a fraction, interpret data in table format as parts of a whole, reduce fractions (with approximation), compare fractions, calculate percents and decimals, and construct a reasonably accurate circle graph.

The purposes for my assessment were to (1) understand my students' mathematical thinking, (2) evaluate their responses using a R/M rubric, and (3) guide future instructional decisions. I used the simple two-part general holistic rubric that follows.

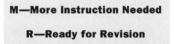

M—More Instruction Needed

R—Ready for Revision

The flowchart in figure 4.6 illustrates the way I analyze a set of a student's work.

FIG. 4.6

USING THE R/M SPLIT RUBRIC

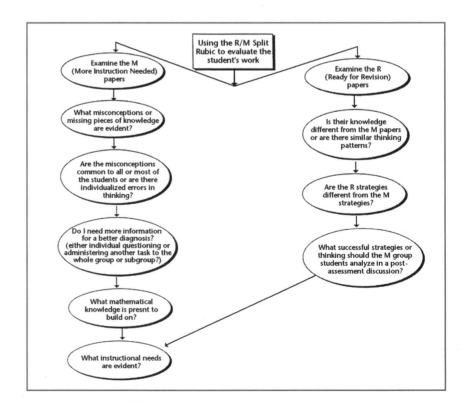

Scoring Student Work

FIG. 4.7

BASKETBALL OR BASEBALL TASK AND STUDENT WORK

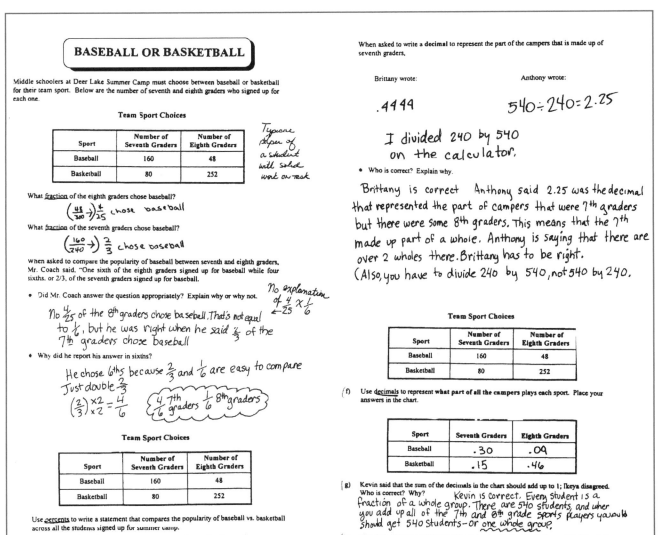

BASEBALL OR BASKETBALL

Middle schoolers at Deer Lake Summer Camp must choose between baseball or basketball for their team sport. Below are the number of seventh and eighth graders who signed up for each one.

Team Sport Choices

Sport	Number of Seventh Graders	Number of Eighth Graders
Baseball	160	48
Basketball	80	252

Typical paper of a student will solid work on task

What fraction of the eighth graders chose baseball?

$\left(\frac{48}{300}\rightarrow\right)\frac{4}{25}$ chose baseball

What fraction of the seventh graders chose baseball?

$\left(\frac{160}{240}\rightarrow\right)\frac{2}{3}$ chose baseball

When asked to compare the popularity of baseball between seventh and eighth graders, Mr. Coach said, "One sixth of the eighth graders signed up for baseball while four sixths, or 2/3, of the seventh graders signed up for baseball.

• Did Mr. Coach answer the question appropriately? Explain why or why not.

No explanation of $\frac{4}{25}\times\frac{1}{6}$

No $\frac{4}{25}$ of the 8th graders chose baseball. That's not equal to $\frac{1}{6}$, but he was right when he said $\frac{2}{3}$ of the 7th graders chose baseball

• Why did he report his answer in sixths?

He chose 6ths because $\frac{2}{3}$ and $\frac{1}{6}$ are easy to compare Just double $\frac{2}{3}$

$\left(\frac{2}{3}\right)\times 2=\frac{4}{6}$ $\frac{4}{6}$ 7th graders $\frac{1}{6}$ 8th graders

Team Sport Choices

Sport	Number of Seventh Graders	Number of Eighth Graders
Baseball	160	48
Basketball	80	252

Use percents to write a statement that compares the popularity of baseball vs. basketball across all the students signed up for summer camp.

39% of the students chose baseball and 61% of the students chose basketball

When asked to write a decimal to represent the part of the campers that is made up of seventh graders,

Brittany wrote: Anthony wrote:

.4444 $540\div240=2.25$

I divided 240 by 540 on the calculator.

• Who is correct? Explain why.

Brittany is correct. Anthony said 2.25 was the decimal that represented the part of campers that were 7th graders but there were some 8th graders. This means that the 7th made up part of a whole. Anthony is saying that there are over 2 wholes there. Brittany has to be right. (Also, you have to divide 240 by 540, not 540 by 240.

Team Sport Choices

Sport	Number of Seventh Graders	Number of Eighth Graders
Baseball	160	48
Basketball	80	252

(f) Use decimals to represent what part of all the campers plays each sport. Place your answers in the chart.

Sport	Seventh Graders	Eighth Graders
Baseball	.30	.09
Basketball	.15	.46

(g) Kevin said that the sum of the decimals in the chart should add up to 1; Ikeya disagreed. Who is correct? Why? Kevin is correct. Every student is a fraction of a whole group. There are 540 students, and when you add up all of the 7th and 8th grade sports players you would should get 540 students—or one whole group.

(h) The circle below is divided into 10 equal parts. **Estimate, shade, and label** the circle graph to represent the portion of all campers who are:

• seventh graders signed up for baseball,

• seventh graders signed up for basketball,

• eighth graders signed up for baseball, and

• eighth graders signed up for basketball.

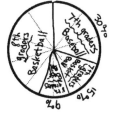

Scoring Student Work

The discussion below shows how I separated R responses from M responses.

SEPARATING M AND R WORK

Part I—Separating R from M

A "Ready for Revision (**R**)" response must either accomplish the task or provide convincing evidence of the mathematical power to do so.

The key issues are *writing a fraction to interpret data as a part of a whole* and *reducing and comparing fractions.*

An **R** response....

■ Writes fractions as part of whole correctly using the original numbers.

■ Shows understanding that 48/300 is close to 50/300 = 1/6 or states that 4/25 does not equal 1/6.

■ Demonstrates understanding that 160/240 = 2/3 or shows simplifying of fractions.

■ Part C—

   1. Takes a position and defends it using correct mathematical reasoning in Part 1.

   2. Makes reference to a common factor of six or gives any reasonable answer using a comparison or states that it is easier in real life for Part 2.

Overall, an **R** response provides evidence that the student could independently revise the response to accomplish the task with minimal feedback, such as a note or focusing question.

If the reader is not confident that a note to the student would suffice to elicit a revision that accomplishes the task, the response is a "More Instruction Needed (**M**)."

Part II—Separating R from M

A "Ready for Revision (**R**)" response must either accomplish the task or provide convincing evidence of the mathematical power to do so.

The key issues are *calculating percents and decimals and interpreting as part of a whole* and *reasonably accurate circle graph that is completely filled and correct as to relative sizes.*

An **R** response....

■ Correctly calculates decimals, percents, and interprets as part of a whole.

■ Presents a reasonably accurate circle graph that is completely filled and correct as to relative size.

■ Leaves no more than one part incomplete if everything else is correct.

   1. If there is a mistake in one part of the answer, the remainder of the work needs to show sufficient understanding of the mathematics that the scorer feels confident that the student could make the necessary correction without further help.

Overall, an **R** response provides evidence that the student could independently revise the response to accomplish the task with minimal feedback, such as a note or focusing questions. If the reader is not confident that a note to the student would suffice to elicit a revision that accomplishes the task, the response is a "More Instruction Needed (**M**)."

CHAPTER *4*

Scoring Student Work

My conclusions about my students' work on this task are summarized below.

ANALYSIS

In examining the students' work, it became evident that students' understanding of fractions was not necessarily correlated with the decimal and percent portions of the task, so I analyzed their work in two parts.

Part I Analysis

■ There was a common misconception in students' work scored both **M** and **R** that was focused on the statement "One sixth of the eighth graders signed up for baseball." An overwhelming majority of the students did not recognize the fraction 4/25 as being close enough to 1/6 to justify the statement. Instructionally, I know that I need to do more work with estimation of fractions with the whole class. I will also try the addition of the words "about" or "approximately" to the prompt next administration to see if the prompt itself was misleading.

■ There was also a problem with many students not being able to access the correct numbers from the 2×2 table. This can be attributed to students not being able to distinguish the part from the whole and inexperience with this format. Both these possible explanations can be handled instructionally.

Part II Analysis

■ Most students were computationally proficient on parts (d) and (f) but many of the students receiving an **M** were unable to explain their thinking in parts (e) and (g). I must provide more opportunities for students to explain their thinking in writing since the explanations and discourse in class seemed to indicate an understanding of the part-whole relationship that did not translate into a written explanation.

■ The construction of the circle graph was mastered by all students even if they were using the wrong numbers.

■ I was unsure if the students who simply added the correct decimal representations in part (f) understood what they did. I noted that they did in fact add to one or very close to one, without an adequate explanation of the relationship of the sum of the parts to the whole.

■ Many students receiving an "**M**" analyzed the results in part (f) separately for grades 7 and 8 so that each part added to 1. They then devised an overlapping system for their circle graphs. I thought that by using **BOLD** on "what part of all the campers," I could circumvent this problem.

Scoring Student Work

TIPS FROM TEACHERS

■ *Make sure students understand the rubric and distribute it ahead of time.*

■ *Choose an easy problem to start so that there is little confusion about quality work. Guide scoring decisions by handing out examples of each performance level. These are called anchor papers, and they come from other classes or previous classes.*

■ *Select model pieces from the class to show solid scores at different points to help calibrate the class and validate their initial scores.*

■ *Have students share their work, score each other's work, and defend the scores they have assigned.*

■ *Select random work and ask students to score it. Ask them to justify their scores. Remove student names from the work.*

■ *Ask students to create samples of work for a particular task that would earn each of the scores in the rubric.*

READ ABOUT...

■ *Read about the concerns a group of teachers have with their students scoring work using a teacher-designed rubric in "A Difference of Opinion" in* Mathematics Assessment: Cases and Discussion Questions for Grades 6–12 *(Bush 2000).*

■ *Read about teachers' problems in agreeing on criteria for scoring student work in "Right or Wrong" in* Mathematics Assessment: Cases and Discussion Questions for Grades 6–12 *(Bush 2000).*

HOW CAN I GET STUDENTS TO SCORE THEIR OWN WORK?

Scoring all of our students' work is time-consuming. It is helpful if our students can learn to assess their work themselves. This practice also has the added benefit of giving students the chance to assess themselves and their peers.

As we use rubrics regularly in our assessment, our students become more comfortable with them. They also realize how much time and thought goes into quality work. They are ready to score their own work as well as the work of others. Most students are capable of accurately and reliably scoring their own work, but we will need to spend some time helping them learn. The box on the left contains some tips offered by other teachers to help get students ready to score their own work.

HOW CAN I CONVERT STUDENT SCORES AND RATINGS TO GRADES?

The answer to this question can be simple. If report card grades are summaries or averages—weighted or not weighted—of a set of scores or smaller grades, then converting holistic or analytical scores to grades involves the same weighted or unweighted averaging process.

With previous assessment, we computed grades by averaging quiz, test, and possibly homework grades—each representing a percent of items correct or total number of points. With additional types of assessment, we average scores of 4, 3, 2, and 1. We can take into account the scores of larger projects by doubling or tripling these scores. In the past, supporting evidence for grades came primarily from quiz and test scores. Under a more balanced assessment system, grades are supported with samples of students' work and can be collected in a portfolio.

Figure 4.8 illustrates a copy of a grade book page from a teacher who uses different scoring strategies.

CHAPTER *4*

Scoring Student Work

FIG. 4.8

A TEACHER'S GRADE BOOK

Math All — 2nd Progress Report

NAMES	Equivalent Fractions	Bonny's Ratio 4	Landsers Plot	Pie Graph of my time Mrs. Keller	Individualized Work	Mad Min 60	Favorite Sports outside Circle
Jesse	A / A	✓ Explained		✓+A	10/12	49 A 5.35	12/12 A / ✓ B
Magen	✓ B			✓+A		50/50 4.50	10/12 B / ✓ B
Evan	✓ B					41 4.50 50 B	12/12 A / ✓+A
Brandon	✓+A			✓+A	8/8 6/6 16/16	47 B 3:00 50	12/12 A / ✓+A
Kristen	✓ B			✓+A	8/8 2/6 16/16	42 B 4:55 50	12/12 A / ✓+A
Melodie	✓ B	Very Weak piece	B	✓		44 B 6:00 50	10/12 B / ⊘
Zachary	✓ B		B	✓+A	7/8 5/6 4/16	52 A 2:35 50	12/12 A / ✓ B
Debbie	✓ D	✓ Great		✓+A		49 B 2:45	12/12 A / ✓ B
Jessica	✓ B	✓ Excellent great	✓ B	A 12/12	48 B 2:45 50	12/12 A / ✓+A
Tori	✓+A	✓ Excellent		✓+A	8/8 6/6 16/16	49 A .58 50	12/12 A / ✓ B
Sam	✓+A +5		B	✓+	@	With Ms B.	@ / ✓+A
Loren	✓ D	✓+ Great	A	✓+A	8/8 5/6 16/16	48 2.50 50	12/12 A / @
Erinn	✓+A	✓+		✓+A		50 A.15 50	12/12 A / ✓ B
Caitlin	✓+A		B	✓+A	@	49 A.55 50	12/12 A / ✓ B
Adam	✓+A +3			✓ sloppy	12/12	52 A 4:00 50	1/2 A / ✓+A
Chris	✓ D	great ideas. Need to illustrate more		✓		With Ms. B.	@
Russell	⊘		B	✓	8/8 6/6 16/16	49 2:20 50	12/12 A / ✓+
Meredith	✓+A	Needed to draw		✓+A		50 3.25 50 A	12/12 A / ✓
Ryan	✓+A	✓+ are A finished!	A	✓	8/8 3/6 16/16	50 2:35 50	12/12 A / ✓
Sarah	✓ B	✓+	B	✓+A	8/8 6/6 16/16	50 2:20 50	12/12 A / @
Joey	N/A	N/A	N/A	N/A	N/A	N/A	N/A / N/A
Seth	✓				8/8 4/6 16/16	With drawn	

Scoring Student Work

READ ABOUT...

■ *Read about a middle school teacher's struggle with grading in "Does This Count for a Grade?" in* Mathematics Assessment: Cases and Discussion Questions for Grades 6–12 *(Bush 2000).*

■ *For more tips about grading, read* Mathematics Assessment: Myths, Models, Good Questions, and practical Suggestions, *edited by Jean Stenmark (1991).*

SOMETHING TO THINK ABOUT

Subjectivity in scoring problem-solving tasks has proved difficult for mathematics teachers. Yet, English teachers seem to have little difficulty in objectively scoring student writing. Talk to an English teacher in your school about the way he/she tries to avoid subjectivity in scoring student work.

HOW CAN I BE ASSURED THAT I SCORE STUDENT WORK CONSISTENTLY AND RELIABLY?

Scoring samples of students' writing and problem-solving performance requires more judgment than scoring tasks that have one right answer. Making sure that our scores reflect judgments that are consistent among students and over time is important if the scores are to be meaningful.

One solution to the problem is to work with other teachers. Scoring students' work together over time will lead to more consistent and reliable results. Using rubrics that clearly delineate students' performance is also helpful. Teachers who believe that their scoring has become consistent offer the following advice:

■ *Use fewer categories in the rubric. It is easier to be consistent with four categories than it is with ten categories.*

■ *Always read several students' responses before developing a rubric. Try to look for a variety of responses.*

■ *Never look at students' names while scoring their work.*

■ *Read quickly through all papers before reading each carefully.*

■ *Our mathematics department meets regularly to score students' work together. We always learn something when we do this, and it helps us be more consistent as a department.*

Making Instructional Decisions

HOW CAN I USE STUDENT WORK GATHERED DURING ASSESSMENT TO MAKE MORE INFORMED INSTRUCTIONAL DECISIONS?

Assessment results can guide our teaching on two levels. Broadly, they help us plan curricula, units, activities, and subsequent assessment. These results also help us shape our classroom environment to foster learning and positive experiences. Diana Lambdin and Clare Forseth (1996) offer a set of questions based on the NCTM *Assessment Standards for School Mathematics* to help us shape our practice:

- How does the mathematics of this assessment/instruction fit within the framework of important mathematics? (Mathematics Standard)

- How does the mathematics of this assessment/instruction contribute to student's learning mathematics? (Learning Standard)

- What opportunities does each student have to engage in the assessment/instruction? (Equity Standard)

- How have students become familiar with the assessment/instruction and its purposes, expectations, and consequences? (Openness Standard)

- How are multiple sources of evidence being used for drawing inferences that lead to assessment/instructional decisions? (Inferences Standard)

- How does this assessment/instruction match specific goals? (Coherence Standard)

Another important result of assessment is making informed daily decisions, including whether or not to reteach a topic or how to teach a topic differently. The assessment results we obtain through observations, interviews, or examinations of students' work help us decide what to do next.

The following are some questions we might ask ourselves as we think about what we will do next:

- Was the overall quality of students' work poor enough to suggest problems with my teaching? If so, how can it be fixed?

- Was the overall quality of the work high enough to suggest success? If so, what is a logical next step?

- Did some or many students miss important prerequisite skills or concepts? If so, what material needs to be retaught?

- Were my standards and expectations clear to students? If not, how can my expectations be more explicit?

- Did all students have access to materials and resources? If not, how should access be given?

- Were students motivated? If not, how should my classroom environment or the context of the task be improved?

Careful analysis of our student work often allows us to better understand our own teaching. Our new assessment allows us to better probe the underlying reasons—mathematical, pedagogical, motivational, and environmental—that both explain what happened and point us toward improvement next time.

Giving Feedback to Students

HOW CAN I GIVE USEFUL FEEDBACK TO MY STUDENTS?

One of the strongest arguments for using many types of assessment is that they enable teachers to give students meaningful feedback about their mathematical understanding and their effort. This feedback, in turn, enhances their learning. Think about the information about students that is based on observations, interviews, journals, projects, and portfolios as opposed to information based on tests, quizzes, and homework. Compare the feedback, "You got three wrong," with the comment, "Nice work, your graphs are clear and accurate, but the conclusions you draw from the data are incomplete and rather superficial."

Effective feedback for students requires that they have a clear understanding of the task and of the rubric, checklist, or expectations being used to score the task. The list in the left column offers some common tools used to provide feedback.

In **figure 4.9** is a set of criteria for providing feedback recommended by the Math Learning Center.

READ MORE ABOUT IT

■ *Read about a teacher's concern with communicating assessment results to her students in "How Do I Assess Thee? Let Me Count the Ways" in* Mathematics Assessment: Cases and Discussion Questions for Grades K–5 *(Bush 2001).*

FIG. 4.9

CRITERIA FOR JOURNAL FEEDBACK (MATH LEARNING CENTER)

> **WHAT TO EMPHASIZE IN YOUR JOURNAL**
>
> When you write in your journal, remember to record the problem or question you are writing about so that your entry will make sense when you or your teacher reads it later. Be sure to date each journal entry. Emphasize the following in your journal entries:
>
> ■ mathematical communication (describe your understanding of concepts and your methods or ideas in words, diagrams, and math symbols)
>
> ■ mathematical reasoning (whenever possible, support your ideas with logical arguments)
>
> ■ your own solutions to math problems and ideas you get from others
>
> ■ your conjectures and generalizations
>
> ■ your AHA!s and "lightbulb" moments
>
> ■ your feelings (joy, disequilibrium, excitement, confidence, worries, etc.)
>
> ■ your questions and math ideas you wonder about
>
> ■ ways your thinking about a math concept or procedure has changed
>
> ■ connections you notice among math ideas, between math and other subjects, and between math and your life outside of school
>
> Regularly review your journal. When you do this, write a new journal entry describing the mathematical growth, strengths, and needs you notice.
>
> It is important not to erase a journal entry, even if you feel what you wrote before is wrong. Instead, show growth by adding new ideas (write the date that you make the addition). Or, on another page describe how your thinking has changed.

CHAPTER *4*

Giving Feedback to Students

Figures **4.10** and **4.11** illustrate two other tools to provide feedback on observations and on portfolios.

FIG. 4.10

MATH TASKS OBSERVATION GUIDELINES

Math TASKS Observation Guideline MS 6-7-8	Group / Individual / Pairs

Problem Title: _____
or Task Title: _____

Group	
Individual	
Pairs	

Focus Areas   **Comments**

1. How does the student get started on a problem?
    a) Asks other student   **c)** Self starts
    b) Asks teacher   **d)** Does nothing

2. What does the student do to get "unstuck?"
    a) Asks teacher   **c)** Copies other student
    b) Asks other student   **d)** Gives up

3. What kinds of questions does the student ask?
    a) Cop-out (i.e., "I don't understand any of it.")
    b) Irrelevant   **c)** Clarifying question/partial understanding

4. What methods do they use to do the problem?
    a) Problem-solving strategies   **c)** Discussion with other student
    b) Tools (appropriate/inappropriate) ruler, pencil, paper, calculator

5. Work Habits
    a) Initiative   **d)** Works individually/pairs/cooperatively
    b) Perseverance   **e)** On task
    c) Resourcefulness

Additional Information:
    Attendance   Citizenship   Completion of assignments

FIG. 4.11

PORTFOLIO EVALUATION

PORTFOLIO EVALUATION   **GIVE REASONS FOR EACH RATING**
Rate each category 0–4, 4=great, 3=good, 2=fair or OK, 1=inadequate, 0=missing

Name of student on portfolio_____   Date_____

Category	Rating	Reason
1. Is the portfolio attractive and neat? (title page)		
2. Is the portfolio complete and orderly? (table of contents)		
3. Is the work selected appropriate? (quality potential?)		
4. What is the quality of work selected?		
5. Are evaluations and descriptions thoughtful and thorough?		
6. Self-evaluation and letter to reader		
TOTAL POINTS (24 possible)		Evaluator's Name:

Other comments:

Communicating to Parents

TIPS FROM TEACHERS

■ *Try to let parents know specific goals for assessment. Send a letter home at the beginning of the year.*

■ *Explain the type of homework that will be given and show examples of open-ended questions or projects the children might bring home.*

■ *Describe the grading system to parents because it is quite different than the ones they had in school.*

■ *Provide parents a specific list of suggestions explaining how to help their children with their assignments.*

■ *Require the students to make presentations to their parents about what they know and can do.*

HOW CAN I BEST REPORT THE RESULTS OF MY ASSESSMENT TO PARENTS AND OTHERS?

Communicating with parents and other caregivers about our goals for assessment, how we have set up our classroom assessment system, and the types of assessments we use invites them to be part of the process. Unfortunately, most parents and caregivers are unfamiliar with the types of assessment discussed in this book. It is important that we give them the opportunity to understand the changes occurring at the classroom, state, and national levels.

Figures 4.12, **4.13**, and **4.14** illustrate three parent letters written by teachers to communicate assessment results to their students' parents. Compare the styles and information provided in each letter.

The items in the "Tips from Teachers" columns are some ideas teachers have used for communicating with parents.

FIG. 4.12

PARENT LETTER 1

Dear Parents/Guardians.

As we begin this school year. I want to share with you some insights into what is happening in our math classroom. Communication between home and school is very important for you and especially your son/daughter.

Since it seems things are a bit different since you and I were in school, I would like to share some of the goals for the class and expectations that I have of your son or daughter.

Here are the goals:

1. To communicate mathematically through
   ■ Representation (graphs, diagrams, charts, tables, etc.)
   ■ Math language
   ■ Clear presentation of work
2. To demonstrate problem solving by
   ■ Showing understanding of the tasks
   ■ Using approaches, sometimes more than one, that show good sound mathematical thinking.
   ■ Explaining decisions along the way
   ■ Connecting, extending, applying, and generalizing answers
3. To develop number sense by
   ■ Assessing when an answer is reasonable
   ■ Using mental strategies to do computation and estimation
4. To understand and apply math skills and concepts
5. To solve problems cooperatively
6. To apply math outside the classroom
7. To use technology to facilitate problem solving
8. To grow in self-esteem and self-confidence as a person and as a mathematician

CHAPTER *4*

Communicating to Parents

FIG. 4.12 (CONTINUED)

PARENT LETTER 1

Here are the expectations

1. Daily homework that should take between 20 and 40 minutes (some shorter, some longer.) You should be able to say, "That's enough," and write a brief note saying you felt your son or daughter had spent adequate time.

2. The homework is not traditional textbook homework but questions that require a lot of thought and explanation on the part of the student.

3. I expect that sometimes your son or daughter will get frustrated. I am trying to teach them that math is not always an "answer" but a thought process, and sometimes the work turned in might be methods tried that didn't necessarily work or questions that they might have to get further in the problem.

4. Tests and quizzes are about once every two weeks.

5. Journal entries will be on the off-test weeks.

6. Your child will learn to score his or her own work, assess him or herself, and discuss a grade for the marking period with me.

Here are some suggestions that will enable you to share in your child's experiences in learning mathematics and help you to create an environment in your home that provides encouragement for your child.

■ Show interest in your child's experience in math class. Ask him or her to tell you about class activities and show interest in them.

■ Ask your child to explain the concepts and relationships he or she is studying. Be concerned with the process as well as the answer. Let him or her explain his or her thoughts to you often.

■ When your child has a question, try not to tell him or her how to solve the problem. Ask questions that will help him or her think about the problem in a different way.

■ Encourage your child to draw diagrams, models, or sketches to help explain or understand a concept or problem.

■ Provide a special time or place for study that will not be disrupted by other household activities.

■ Encourage your child to form study groups with classmates. By discussing concepts with others, rich insights will emerge.

■ Engage your child in home activities that draw on a variety of mathematical skills. Games and puzzles, estimations, and math talk at meal time are good ways to do this.

■ Come and visit your child's math class.

The goals and expectations are strongly related to the National Council of Teachers of Mathematics *Curriculum and Evaluation Standards for School Mathematics (1989)*. Teaching math where kids are involved in the process makes math more meaningful and useful. Students will see that it isn't "magic" but they will know why and how things work.

I'm looking forward to seeing you at open house. Let me know if you have any questions or concerns. I'm excited about the school year ahead and look forward to working with your child.

Sincerely,

TIPS FROM TEACHERS

■ *Send home a monthly newsletter containing information about the mathematics classroom, highlighting a different component of the assessment system each time.*

■ *Send home homework for parents to do together with their children. Include a form where the parent writes responses to questions such as "What mathematics did you use to solve these problems?"*

■ *Have parents read the child's portfolio at home and write comments about it.*

■ *Invite parents to mathematics workshops.*

■ *Ask parents to help score papers.*

■ *As part of Open House or Math Night, conduct a workshop about the types of mathematics problems and assessment strategies you are using.*

■ *Show parents the types of items that are on "high-stakes" tests, especially open-ended and essay questions.*

Communicating to Parents

READ ABOUT...

■ *Read about teachers whose students communicate assessment results to their parents in "Math Portfolio Night" in* Mathematics Assessment: Cases and Discussion Questions for Grades 6–12 *(Bush 2000) and in "Student-Led Conferences" in* Mathematics Assessment: Cases and Discussion Questions for Grades K–5 *(Bush 2001).*

■ *Read about a teacher whose revised rubric enabled her to better communicate with parents in "Accountability" in* Mathematics Assessment: Cases and Discussion Questions for Grades K–5 *(Bush 2001)*

FIG. 4.13

PARENT LETTER 2

Dear Parents,

This letter is to update you on the next unit your child will be studying in math class. The unit is called **Shapes and Designs**. It is a unit on geometry that is intended to help students learn about the many geometric figures that arise in the world around us. Studying the mathematics underlying shapes and designs will help your child build an understanding of why different shapes or designs are useful. The mathematical and problem-solving goals of the unit are these:

- ■ Understanding what a polygon is
- ■ Understanding how the lengths of edges determine the shape and uses of polygons
- ■ Understanding how the sizes of angles determine the shape and uses of polygons
- ■ Understanding and using angle measurement
- ■ Moving from recognition of shapes to classification of shapes to analysis of shapes
- ■ Observing and describing shapes as they are used in the world

Exploring and using these mathematical ideas will help your child begin to develop an understanding of geometry that connects mathematics to the surrounding world. Please contact me if you have any questions or concerns.

Sincerely,

CHAPTER *4*

FIG. 4.14

PARENT LETTER 3

Dear_____,

Attached you will find _____'s growth-folio, which contains several important assignments and activities selected from this term's work in math. Please set aside about 30 minutes to have _____ *present to you* the eight items in this growth-folio (each item has a colored quarter-sheet of paper attached to the front). Then write a short note at the bottom of this page reacting to the work demonstrated.

Please keep in mind that learning to make in-depth self-assessments of one's work takes time. For many of the students, this is their first experience analyzing their own efforts and achievements and looking for evidence to support their analyses. The attached sheets, "Evidence I'm Growing I and II," describe what the students and I watch for as indicators they are growing as mathematicians. I encourage you to point out evidence of growth that you notice during your child's presentation.

The students will add to their growth-folios next term and repeatedly throughout the year. Each term you will be asked to listen to a growth-folio presentation. By the end of the year, this should provide a broad picture of your child's mathematical achievements, understanding, and growth.

Please call me at _____ if you have any questions.

Respectfully,

My child explained each of the eight items in this growth-folio to me. Some reactions that I have are: _____

_____

_____

_____

_____

_____

_____

_____

_____
Signature(s) of Parent(s) or Guardian(s)

Please return this note and growth-folio to school by _____

Chapter 5

Exemplary Mathematics Assessment Tasks for the Middle Grades

Samantha's Grades

Samantha made the following scores on unit tests for the term: 92, 98, 15, 92, 87, 92. Samantha's teacher said her grades would be based on the mean of her grades. Samantha argued that her grade should be based on the median of her grades.

1. Find the mean and median of Samantha's grades.

2. Which do you think best reflects Samantha's work for the term? Explain your reasoning.

Grade 8 Open-Response Item from the 1993–94 Kentucky Instructional Results Information System. Reprinted with permission from the Kentucky Department of Education. Please note that KIRIS has been replaced by the Commonwealth Accountability Testing System.

Sports Bag

Each bag has the shape of a cylinder and is described below:

- The body of the bag is 60 cm long.

- The circular ends have a diameter of 25 cm.

- The body is made from a single rectangular piece of heavy fabric.

- The ends are each made from a circular piece of the same kind of fabric. (That makes three pieces altogether: one body, two ends.)

- Remember to add an extra 2 cm all around each piece to allow the pieces to be stitched together.

- The strapping will be cut from different material, created and put together by a different department, so you do not need to worry about it.

CIRCLE REMINDER:

Diameter (*d*) goes all the way across.

Radius (*r*) is the distance from the center to the outside of the circle.

Use *pi* (π) = 3.14.

The circumference (the distance around) is $C = 2\pi r$ or $C = \pi d$.

The area is $A = \pi r^2$.

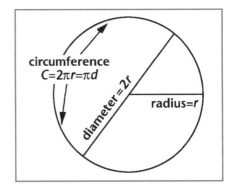

You will cut the three pieces of your bag from fabric that comes on a long roll. This roll is 100 cm wide.

1. What is the shortest length that you need to cut from the roll to have enough fabric for one bag? **Draw a diagram** showing how the three pieces will be cut from the roll. Explain your thinking.

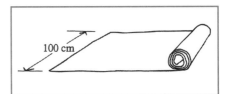

2. What is the shortest length that you would need to cut from the same fabric roll to have enough fabric for three bags? **Draw a diagram** of how the pieces will be cut from the roll and label the dimensions of the pieces. Make sure to explain what you did and how you did it.

Emergency 911! Heights City

Last week there was an accident at the Waterfront Amusement Park in Heights City. A seat on one of the rides broke loose, resulting in serious injury for two teenagers. The owners of the amusement park have charged that if the ambulances had responded more quickly, the injuries of the two teens would have been less severe. They have charged in the newspapers that Heights City 911 Emergency Service failed to dispatch ambulances efficiently.

The Heights City Emergency Service manager wants to conduct an internal investigation of his company's response times to the area of the amusement park in order to establish a policy for operators to follow. They have hired you to investigate the data they have collected over the last month that indicates the time of day and the length of response time for the two ambulance companies in Heights City.

The following letter is sent to you by the Heights City 911 Emergency Service:

Dear Consultant,

Thank you for agreeing to conduct our internal evaluation of the Waterfront Amusement Park response-time problem. We understand that you have agreed to write a report that does the following things:

1. Analyze the response time data from the last month for the two ambulance companies in Heights City. Your analysis should include graphs, numerical summaries, narrative descriptions of your analysis, and so on, that help the owners of Heights City 911 Emergency Service communicate the situation to the news media and public.

2. Write a recommendation to the manager that clearly states which companies to dispatch to the Waterfront Amusement Park during its hours of operation throughout the week. Explain why you made your recommendations. (NOTE: We suspect that the time of day and whether it is a weekend or weekday makes a difference.)

You will find enclosed the information you will need to conduct your evaluation. The information below has important information about the amusement park and about the emergency service. The second page has the log sheet of response times for the month of May.

ABOUT WATERFRONT AMUSEMENT PARK:

- The park is open every day of the week.
- The park is open to the public between the hours of 8 A.M. and 7 P.M.
- Employees begin arriving at the park at 7 A.M. and have cleared out of the park by 8 P.M.

CHAPTER *5*

ABOUT HEIGHTS CITY 911 EMERGENCY SERVICE:

■ There are three shifts of operators: 7 A.M. until 3 P.M.; 3 P.M. until 11 P.M.;
11 P.M. until 7 A.M.

■ The emergency operators can call one of the two companies in Heights
City: Arrow Ambulance Service and Metro Ambulances.

■ The attached log sheet shows the response time of the two companies for
an area within a one-mile radius of Waterfront Amusement Park. (NOTE:
Apparently the response time can take as little as 4 minutes to as long as
19 minutes!) These are the data from the month of May.

■ Response time is defined as the length of time from when a 911 operator
receives an emergency call to when an ambulance arrives on the scene of
an accident.

RESPONSE TIME FOR HEIGHTS CITY AMBULANCES

Date of Call	Time of Call	Company Name	Response Time in minutes
Wed., May 1	7:56 AM	Metro	10
Wed., May 1	2:20 AM	Arrow	11
Wed., May 1	12:41 PM	Arrow	8
Wed., May 1	2:29 PM	Metro	11
Thurs., May 2	8:14 AM	Metro	8
Thurs., May 2	6:23 PM	Metro	16
Fri., May 3	4:15 AM	Metro	7
Fri., May 3	8:41 AM	Arrow	19
Sat., May 4	7:12 AM	Metro	11
Sat., May 4	7:43 PM	Metro	11
Sat., May 4	10:02 PM	Arrow	7
Sun., May 5	12:22 PM	Metro	12
Mon., May 6	6:47 AM	Metro	9
Mon., May 6	7:15 AM	Arrow	16
Mon., May 6	6:10 PM	Arrow	8
Tues., May 7	5:37 PM	Metro	16
Tues., May 7	9:37 PM	Metro	11
Thurs., May 9	5:30 AM	Arrow	17
Thurs., May 9	6:18 PM	Arrow	6
Fri., May 10	6:25 AM	Arrow	16
Sat., May 11	1:03 AM	Metro	12
Mon., May 13	6:40 AM	Arrow	17
Mon., May 13	3:25 PM	Metro	15
Tues., May 14	4:59 PM	Metro	14
Thurs., May 16	10:11 AM	Metro	8
Thurs., May 16	11:45 AM	Metro	10
Fri., May 17	11:09 AM	Arrow	7
Fri., May 17	9:15 PM	Arrow	8
Fri., May 17	11:15 PM	Metro	8
Mon., May 20	7:25 AM	Arrow	17
Mon., May 20	4:20 PM	Metro	19
Thurs., May 23	2:39 PM	Arrow	10
Thurs., May 23	3:44 PM	Metro	14
Fri., May 24	8:56 PM	Metro	10
Sat., May 25	8:30 PM	Arrow	8
Sun., May 26	6:33 AM	Metro	6
Mon., May 27	4:21 PM	Arrow	9
Tues., May 28	8:07 AM	Arrow	15
Tues., May 28	5:02 PM	Arrow	7
Wed., May 29	10:51 AM	Metro	9
Wed., May 29	5:11 PM	Metro	18
Thurs., May 30	4:16 AM	Arrow	10
Fri., May 31	8:59 AM	Metro	11

From *Balanced Assessment for the Mathematics Curriculum: Middle Grades Assessment Package* by Alan Schoenfeld, Hugh
Burkhardt, Phil Daro, Jim Ridgway, Judah Schwartz, and Sandra Wilcox, copyright © 1999 by the Regents of the
University of California. Reprinted by permission of Dale Seymour Publications.

Science Fair

Three middle schools are going to have a science fair. The science fair will be in an auditorium. The amount of space given to each school is based on the number of students. Bret Harte Middle School has about 1000 students, Malcolm X Middle School has about 600 students, and Kennedy Middle School has about 400 students.

1. The rectangle below represents the auditorium. Divide the rectangle to show the amount of space each school should get on the basis of number of students. Label each section BH for Bret Harte, MX for Malcolm X, or K for Kennedy.

2. What *fraction* of the space should each school get on the basis of the number of students? Show your mathematical reasoning.

3. If the schools share the cost of the science fair on the basis of the number of students, what percent of the cost should each school pay?

4. If the cost of the science fair is $300.00, how much should each school pay on the basis of number of students? Justify your answers.

Released by New Standards™. Reprinted with permission from New Standards™. The New Standards™ assessment system includes performance standards with performance descriptions, student work samples and commentaries, on-demand examinations, and a portfolio system. For more information contact the National Center on Education and the Economy, 202-783-3668 or www.ncee.org.

Pet Confusion

Lynn and Bill are planning a joint project. They decide to write an article for their school newspaper on the number of pets in a typical household of members of the Future Veterinarians Club. They ask the following question of each club member:

- "How many pets live in your house?"

Featured to the right are the results of the survey.

Design a way to organize and display the data for Lynn and Bill's newspaper article.

Lynn and Bill disagree about the best headline for the article. Lynn's headline was:

> **Holy Cow!**
>
> **TYPICAL FUTURE VETERINARIANS CLUB**
>
> **MEMBER HAS 15 PETS!!!!**

Bill's headline was:

> **PET LOVERS???**
>
> **TYPICAL FUTURE VETERINARIANS CLUB**
>
> **MEMBER HAS 4 PETS!!!**

Both Lynn and Bill are mathematically correct.

- Explain how **both** Lynn and Bill could use mathematics to justify their headlines.

NAME	NUMBER OF PETS
Maria	97
Diane	4
Adrienne	0
Jan	7
Agnes	1
Betsy	9
Todd	0
Maureen	42
Dave	4
Connie	1
Sally	4
Mike	4
Marianne M.	9
Ande	1
Darlene	7
Fedelis	22
Barb	78
Hal	0
Sue	4
Marianne O.	6

- Which headline would you use and why?

Developed by teachers in the Pittsburgh Public Schools. Reprinted with permission from the Unit of Teaching, Learning and Assessment of the Pittsburgh Public Schools.

Wendy's Wish

You are the Public Relations Manager for Wendy's International. You receive this letter from an upset stockholder:

To Whom It May Concern:

I read in the newspaper that Wendy's goal is to have 2 percent of all Americans eat at Wendy's each day. That goal is impossible! There are about 250 million Americans and only 4400 Wendy's restaurants. As a stockholder, I am very concerned that time and money are being wasted on an impossible goal!

As public relations manager, you know it is possible for 2 *percent* of all Americans to eat at Wendy's each day, considering the number of hours Wendy's restaurants are open and the number of serving lines in each restaurant.

Write a letter that uses mathematics to explain to the stockholder that this is possible.

Developed by teachers in the Pittsburgh Public Schools. Reprinted with permission from the Unit of Teaching, Learning and Assessment of the Pittsburgh Public Schools.

Activity Bus Argument

In 1996, the activity bus budget for a large middle school was $25 000 out of a total school bus budget of $482 000. For 1997, the figure is $25 500 for activity buses out of a total school bus budget of $492 000. The cost of living is projected to increase 3 percent between 1996 and 1997.

Different people have different reactions to the 1997 budget:

- Some teachers complain that the money spent on activity buses **increased**.

- The activities director for the school complains that the money for the activity buses has **decreased**.

- The principal maintains that, in fact, there has been **no change** in spending patterns at the school.

Write a paragraph or paragraphs describing how each party (the teachers, the activities director, and the principal) might use mathematics to justify his or her claim.

This task was adapted from a task entitled "Budget Mystery" developed by the Connecticut State Department of Education. It was adapted by teachers in the Pittsburgh Public Schools. Reprinted with permission from Connecticut Department of Education and the Unit of Teaching, Learning and Assessment of the Pittsburgh Public Schools.

Double Discount

At a department store sale, you are buying a $50 sweater that you selected from a table that says "25% OFF." You also have a coupon for an additional 10 percent off any purchase.

Take an additional
10% OFF EVERYTHING
in the store.

Most Merchandise Storewide
Already Reduced 20–50%!

For Example:

Regular price merchandise:	**= $60.00**
Less 25% already discounted:	**= $45.00**
Less additional 10% discount (today):	**= $39.00**

The cashier takes the 25 percent off the original price and then takes an additional 10 percent off. She asks you for $33.75. Write what you would explain to the cashier to justify why this price is not as good as the bargain claimed in the coupon above.

Double the Dotted Line Segment

For each of the figures shown below, draw a new enlarged figure that has the same shape. The dotted line segment in each new figure should be double the length of the dotted line segment in the original figure.

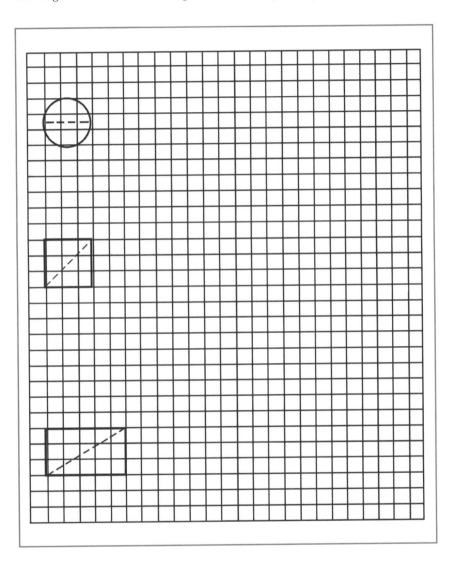

Replanting the Forest

A forest fire has destroyed 3000 trees. To prevent erosion, new trees must be planted. Students from your school want to help replant the forest. Each student is given two trees to plant.

On the first day of replanting, one student plants both of his trees in the forest. On the second day, two students plant their trees. On the third day, four students plant their trees, and so on.

How many days will it take to replant the forest on this schedule?

Explain your plan to the principal so that you can convince her to help get students involved in replanting the forest.

From a "A Sampler of Mathematics Assessment—1994" developed by the California Department of Education.

Lucky Draw? Fund Raiser

At the Palatine School's Fall Fest, the "Charity for Children" Club is planning to run a money-raising booth. One of the members in the club proposed the game in the following box.

Lucky Draw

There are equal numbers of red and blue balls buried in sawdust in each barrel

10¢ PER TURN

One turn allows you to make
ONE LUCKY DRAW from each barrel

Win $1.00

If you draw three balls of the same color on one turn, you win $1.00

Chris, the chairperson of the festival, likes the idea of the game, but she isn't sure whether this is a good moneymaker. You, as co-chair, have been asked to prepare a report to the festival committee on this issue.

Your job is to recommend keeping the game, or to show how to modify it to make it a moneymaker. Support your conclusion with data and reasoning.

From *Balanced Assessment for the Mathematics Curriculum: Middle Grades Assessment Package* by Alan Schoenfeld, Hugh Burkhardt, Phil Daro, Jim Ridgway, Judah Schwartz, and Sandra Wilcox, copyright © 1999 by the Regents of the University of California. Reprinted by permission of Dale Seymour Publications.

How Long Should a Shoelace Be?

Suppose you work for a shoelace company. You receive the following assignment from your boss.

Sports Laces

ASSIGNMENT

We have decided to sell laces for sports shoes. We will sell different lengths for shoes with different numbers of eyelets. We will offer lengths for sports shoes that have 4 eyelets all the way up to 18 eyelets (no odd numbers, of course). No one has ever sold so many different lengths for sports shoes before. You have to figure out what lengths to make and which lengths go with which shoes on the basis of the number of eyelets.

We collected some data from store customers last week. It is confusing because there haven't been very many lengths available. That means that sometimes the customers have had to use lengths that are too short or too long. That's not what we want! We want a unique length for each number of eyelets.

DATA FROM STORE CUSTOMERS WITH SPORTS SHOES

Customer I.D.	Lace Length (inches)	Eyelets (numbers)	Customer I.D.	Lace Length (inches)	Eyelets (numbers)
A	45	8	G	54	12
B	54	10	H	24	4
C	26	4	I	72	14
D	63	14	J	54	12
E	63	12	K	72	16
F	36	8	L	72	18

Write your decisions about lace length so the advertising people making the sign can understand it. They want a table, so customers can look up the number of eyelets and find out the length of lace. They also want a rule, so customers who don't like tables can use the rule to figure out the lengths. Don't worry about making it pretty, they will do that, just make sure the mathematics is right. You better explain how your decisions make sense, so the advertising people will understand.

Thanks.

YOUR BOSS, Angela

Write a response to your boss Angela's assignment that includes the following:

■ A table that shows for each number of eyelets (even numbers only) how long you have decided the laces should be

■ A rule that a customer can use to figure out the length based on the number of eyelets (Don't forget the bow. If you can, express your rule as a formula.)

■ An explanation of your decision (tell why they make sense)

Released by New Standards™. Reprinted with permission from New Standards™. The New Standards™ assessment system includes performance standards with performance descriptions, student work samples and commentaries, on-demand examinations, and a portfolio system. For more information contact the National Center on Education and the Economy, 202-783-3668 or www.ncee.org.

Baseball or Basketball

Middle schoolers at Deer Lake Summer Camp must choose between baseball or basketball for their team sport. To the right are the numbers of seventh and eighth graders who signed up for each one.

Sport	Number of Seventh Graders	Number of Eighth Graders
Baseball	160	48
Basketball	80	252

1. What fraction of the eighth graders chose baseball?

2. What fraction of the seventh graders chose baseball?

3. When asked to compare the popularity of baseball between seventh and eighth graders, Mr. Coach said, "One-sixth of the eighth graders signed up for baseball whereas four-sixths, or 2/3, of the seventh graders signed up for baseball."

■ Did Mr. Coach answer the question appropriately? Explain why or why not.

■ Why did he report his answer in sixths?

4. Use percents to write a statement that compares the popularity of baseball versus basketball across all students signed up for summer camp.

5. When asked to write a decimal to represent the part of the campers that is made up of seventh graders, Brittany and Anthony responded as follows.

Brittany wrote:	Anthony wrote:
.4444 I divided 240 by 540 on the calculator.	540 ÷ 240 = 2.25

Who is correct? Explain why.

6. Use decimals to represent what part of all campers chose each sport. Place your answers in the chart to the right.

7. Kevin said that the sum of the decimals in the chart should add up to 1; Ikeya disagreed. Who is correct? Why?

8. The circle graph to the right is divided into ten equal parts. Estimate, shade, and label the circle graph to represent the portion of all campers who are—

■ seventh graders signed up for baseball;

■ seventh graders signed up for basketball;

■ eighth graders signed up for baseball; and

■ eighth graders signed up for basketball.

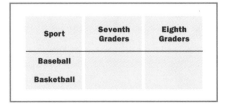

Sport	Seventh Graders	Eighth Graders
Baseball		
Basketball		

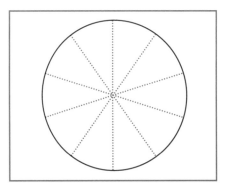

Developed by teachers in the Pittsburgh Public Schools with permission from the Unit of Teaching, Learning and Assessment of the Pittsburgh Public Schools.

Area of an Octagon

How many different ways can you find the area of the regular octagon below with all sides equal to 3 meters? Describe each method and use it to find the area. Are the answers the same? Should they be the same?

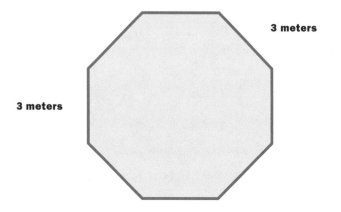

Developed by the San Francisco Unified School District Mentor Teacher Program. Reprinted with permission from the San Francisco Unified School District.

The Family

Imagine a family of five. This imaginary family may be an extended family; that is to say, it may include grandparents, aunts, uncles, and so on. You are one of the five people. The average age of the family is 23 years. Name the other family members and state their relationship to you. Be sure to provide everyone's age (including your own) and explain the mathematics you found it necessary to use.

Developed by the San Francisco Unified School District Mentor Teacher Program. Reprinted with permission from the San Francisco Unified School District.

Softball Team

You are the manager of a softball team. It is the bottom of the ninth inning, two outs are gone, and no one is on base. Your team is one run behind. You plan to send in a pitch hitter in hopes of scoring the tying run. Your possibilities are Joan, Mary, or Bob. Their batting records are given in the table below. Who would you choose to bat? Explain your reasoning.

	Joan	**Mary**	**Bob**
Home Runs	9	15	6
Triples	2	5	3
Doubles	16	11	8
Singles	24	34	18
Walks	11	20	12
Outs	38	85	36

CHAPTER 5

Reprinted with permission by the Connecticut State Department of Education.

Jump Rope

Mrs. Leonard and Mrs. Banister teach sixth-grade mathematics in Pittsburgh. Their classes decided to have a jump rope contest. Students were to jump as many times as they could without stopping or tripping on the rope. The results of each class are given in the tables below.

Mrs. Leonard said that her class did better in the contest. Mrs. Banister disagreed and said her class did better. Mr. Mann, another sixth-grade teacher, looked at the data and said that they both had a mathematical reason for their argument.

1. What mathematical reasoning could Mrs. Leonard use to say that her class was better?

2. What mathematical reasoning could Mrs. Banister use to say that her class was better?

3. Using mathematics, write a paragraph for the student newspaper that will convince the students and both teachers which class you believe did better. You should produce a visual display of the data to help prove your point.

MRS. LEONARD'S CLASS

Student	Score
A. C.	78
A. M.	20
O. T.	2
S. G.	39
M. I.	28
P. T.	29
T. C.	57
D. T.	7
H. A.	8
J. R.	15
C. S.	16
W. T.	16
J. A.	26
M. T.	9
A. T.	18
C. W.	48

MRS. BANISTER'S CLASS

Student	Score
M. R.	51
M. O.	10
K. L.	42
T. S.	41
G. M.	3
I. P.	3
C. D.	31
T. H.	20
A. J.	33
R. C.	4
S. W.	32
T. J.	31
A. M.	28
T. S.	20
T. R.	21
W. S.	30

Developed by teachers in the Pittsburgh Public Schools with permission from the Unit of Teaching, Learning and Assessment of the Pittsburgh Public Schools.

Design Dimensions

Michael and Vonne are designing posters for the antismoking campaign. They want the finished size of the posters to be 24 inches by 36 inches.

Michael has several different sizes of paper he can use to make a rough draft of this poster. Here are the sizes of paper he has to choose from.

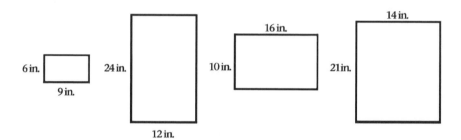

He wants his rough draft to be mathematically similar to the 24″ × 36″ poster. Which sizes of paper could he use? Explain your answer using mathematics.

Vonne decides to use 8″ × 12″ paper to design her poster. By what scale factor will she need to increase her design to fit the 24″ × 36″ paper? Explain your answer.

	8″×12″ Design	24″×36″ Finished Poster
Dimensions of Rectangle	3″ × 7″	
Perimeter		
Area		

Vonne draws a rectangle measuring 3″ × 7″ on her design. What will the measurements of the rectangle on the finished poster be? What will the perimeter and area be? Complete the table on the next page:

If Vonne wants a line to appear 12 inches long on the poster, how long should she make it in her design? Explain you answer using mathematics.

Developed by teachers in the Pittsburgh Public Schools. Reprinted with permission from the Unit of Teaching, Learning and Assessment of the Pittsburgh Public Schools.

CD Sales

At the Blue Moon Recording Company's yearly board meeting, the following chart was presented.

Blue Moon Recording Company Sales Report Pittsburgh Area Sales		
	1993	**1994**
Total Number of CDs sold in Pittsburgh (all record companies combined)	600 000	1 050 000
Number of Blue Moon Recording Company CDs sold in Pittsburgh	200 000	250 000

Reaction was mixed.

The Pittsburgh sales director said:

Great! Our Pittsburgh sales increased.

Disappointing! Considering the total 1994 CD sales, our sales decreased.

The president of the company said:

The statements made by both the sales director and the president are correct from their point of view.

Use mathematics to explain each viewpoint to the Board of Directors.

Developed by teachers in the Pittsburgh Public Schools. Reprinted with permission from the Unit of Teaching, Learning and Assessment of the Pittsburgh Public Schools.

Fair Game

Your friend proposes a game using two cubes, each with faces numbered 1–6. On each roll of the cubes, the resulting numbers on the two "up" faces are multiplied. If the product is even, your friend receives one point. If it is odd, you receive two points. You're not sure this game is fair.

1. Design and conduct an activity to determine whether this game is fair. Explain how you conducted your activity.

2. Describe the results of your activity.

3. Is the game fair? Explain your reasoning using the results of your activity.

4. Is there a fairer way to award points for this game? Explain your reasoning.

CHAPTER 5

Grade 8 Open-Response Item from the 1993–94 Kentucky Instructional Results Information System. Reprinted with permission from the Kentucky Department of Education. Please note that KIRIS has been replaced by the Commonwealth Accountability Testing System.

Resources

Bibliography

Ashlock, Robert. B. *Error Patterns in Computation.* Upper Saddle River, NJ: Prentice Hall, 1998.

Bagley, Theresa, and Catarina Gallenberger. "Assessing Students' Dispositions: Using Journals to Improve Students' Performance." *Mathematics Teacher* 85 (November 1992): 660–63.

Barnett, Carne, Donna Goldenstein, and Babette Jackson. *Fractions, Decimals, Ratios, and Percents: Hard to Teach and Hard to Learn?* Portsmouth, N.H.: Heinemann, 1994.

Bartels, Bobbye H. "Promoting Mathematics Connections with Concept Mapping." *Mathematics Teaching in the Middle School* 1 (November-December 1995): 542–49.

Belcher, Terri, Grace Davila Coates, Jose Franco, and Karen Mayfield-Ingram. "Assessment and Equity." *Multicultural and Gender Equity in the Mathematics Classroom: The Gift of Diversity.* 1997 Yearbook of the National Council of Teachers of Mathematics, edited by Janet Trentacosta, pp. 195–200. Reston, Va: National Council of Teachers of Mathematics, 1997.

Bell, Alan, Rita Crust, Ann Shannon, and Malcolm Swan. *Awareness of Learning, Reflection and Transfer in School Mathematics—Teacher's Handbook.* Nottingham, England: ESRC Project Report R200-23-2329, Shell Centre of Mathematical Education, 1992.

Burns, Marilyn, and Cathy McLaughlin. *A Collection of Math Lessons from Grades 6 through 8.* New Rochelle, N.Y.: Cuisenaire Company of America, 1990.

Bush, William S. (ed.). *Mathematics Assessment: Cases and Discussion Questions for Grades 6–12.* Reston, Va: National Council of Teachers of Mathematics, 2000.

———. *Mathematics Assessment: Cases and Discussion Questions for Grades K–5.* Reston, Va: National Council of Teachers of Mathematics, 2001.

Bush, William S., and Anja S. Greer, eds. *Mathematics Assessment: A Practical Handbook for Grades 9–12.* Reston, Va.: National Council of Teachers of Mathematics, 1999.

California Mathematics Council. *They're Counting On Us.* Sacramento, Calif: California Mathematics Council, 1995.

Center for Education and the Economy. *New Standards Project.* Washington, D.C.: Center for Education and the Economy. <www.ncee.org.>

Chambers, Donald. "Integrating Assessment and Instruction" In *Assessment in the Mathematics Classroom.* 1993 Yearbook of the National Council of

Teachers of Mathematics, edited by Norman L. Webb, pp. 17–25. Reston, Va: National Council of Teachers of Mathematics, 1993.

Charles, Randall, and Frank Lester. *Teaching Problem Solving: What, Why and How*. Palo Alto, Calif.: Dale Seymour Publications, 1982.

Charles, Randall, Frank Lester, and Phares O'Daffer. *How to Evaluate Progress in Problem Solving*. Reston, Va: National Council of Teachers of Mathematics, 1987.

Ciochine, John, and Grace Polivka. "The Missing Link? Writing in Mathematics Class!" *Mathematics Teaching in the Middle School* 2 (March-April 1997): 316–20.

Clarke, David. *Assessment Alternatives in Mathematics*. Canberra, Australia: Curriculum Development Centre, 1988.

———. *Constuctive Assessment in Mathematics: Practical Steps for Classroom Teachers*. Berkeley, Calif.: Key Curriculum Press, 1997.

———. "Quality Mathematics: How Can We Tell?" *Mathematics Teacher* 88 (April 1995): 326-28

Clarke, Doug, and Linda Wilson. "Valuing What We See," *Mathematics Teacher* 87 (October 1994): 542–45.

Crowley, Mary. "Student Mathematics Portfolio: More Than a Display Case." *Mathematics Teacher* 86 (October 1993): 544–47.

Cuevas, Gilbert J. "Developing Communication Skills in Mathematics for Students with Limited English Proficiency." *Mathematics Teacher* 81 (March 1991): 186–89.

Curcio, Frances R., and Alice F. Artz. "Assessing Students' Ability to Analyze Data: Reaching Beyond Computation. *Mathematics Teacher* 89 (November 1996): 668–73.

DiPillo, Mary Lou, Robert Sovchik, and Barbara Moss. "Exploring Middle Graders' Mathematical Thinking through Journals." *Mathematics Teaching in the Middle School* 2 (March-April 1997): 308–14.

Fisher, Lyle, and Bill Midagovich. *Problems of the Week*. Palo Alto, Calif.: Dale Seymour Publications, 1981.

Fleener, M. Jayne, Gloria Nan Dupree, and Lary D. Craven. "Exploring and Changing Visions of Mathematics Teaching and Learning: What Do Students Think?" *Mathematics Teaching in the Middle School* 3 (September 1997): 40–43.

Frank, Martha. "Problem Solving and Mathematical Beliefs." *Arithmetic Teacher* 35 (January 1988): 32–34.

Fuys, David J., and Amy K. Liebov. "Concept Learning in Geometry." *Teaching Children Mathematics* 3 (January 1997): 248–51.

Garofalo, Joe. "Beliefs and Their Influence on Mathematical Performance." *Mathematics Teacher* 82 (October 1989): 502–05.

Gay, Susan, and Margaret Thomas. "Just Because They Got It Right, Does It Mean They Know It?" In *Assessment in the Mathematics Classroom.* 1993 Yearbook of the National Council of Teachers of Mathematics, edited by Norman Webb, pp. 130–34. Reston, Va: National Council of Teachers of Mathematics, 1993.

Kenney, Patricia, and Edward Silver. "Student Self-Assessment in Mathematics." In *Assessment in the Mathematics Classroom.* 1993 Yearbook of the National Council of Teachers of Mathematics, edited by Norman Webb, pp. 229–38. Reston, VA: National Council of Teachers of Mathematics, 1993.

Khisty, Lena L. "Making Mathematics Accessible to Latino Students: Rethinking Instructional Practice" In *Multicultural and Gender Equity in the Mathematics Classroom: The Gift of Diversity.* 1997 Yearbook of the National Council of Teachers of Mathematics, edited by Janet Trentacosta, pp. 92–101. Reston, Va: National Council of Teachers of Mathematics, 1997.

Kroll, Diana L., Joanne O. Masingila, and Sue Tinsley Mau. "Grading Cooperative Problem Solving. *Mathematics Teacher* 85 (November 1992): 619–27.

Kuhs, Teresa. "Portfolio Assessment: Making It Work the First Time." *Mathematics Teacher* 87 (May 1994): 332–35.

Kulm, Gerald. *Mathematics Assessment: What Works in the Classroom.* San Francisco: Jossey-Bass, 1994.

Lambdin, Diana V., and Clare Forseth. "Seamless Assessment/Instruction=Good Teaching." *Teaching Children Mathematics* 2 (January 1996): 294–98.

Lambdin, Diana V., Paul E. Kehle, and Ronald V. Preston, eds. *Emphasis on Assessment: Readings from NCTM's School-Based Journals.* Reston, Va: National Council of Teachers of Mathematics, 1996.

Lambdin, Diana V., and Vicki L. Walker. "Planning for Classroom Portfolio Assessment." *Arithmetic Teacher* 6 (February 1994): 318–24.

Lappan, Glenda, James T. Fey, William M. Fitzgerald, Susan N. Friel, and Elizabeth Phillips. *Connected Mathematics.* Menlo Park, Calif.: Dale Seymour Publications, 1998.

MacGregor, Mollie. "Reading and Writing in Mathematics." In *Language in Mathematics,* edited by Jennie Bickmore-Brand, pp. 100–108. Portsmouth, N.H.: Heinemann, 1993.

Math Learning Center, P.O. Box 3226, Salem, OR 97302; (503) 370-8130.

Mathematical Sciences Education Board. *Measuring What Counts: A Conceptual Guide for Mathematics Assessment.* Washington, D.C.: National Academy Press, 1993.

McIntosh, Margaret. "No Time for Writing in Your Class?" *Mathematics Teacher* 84 (September 1991): 423–33.

National Council of Teachers of Mathematics. *Assessment in the Mathematics Classroom.* 1993 Yearbook of the National Council of Teachers of Mathematics, edited by Norman L. Webb. Reston, Va.: National Council of Teachers of Mathematics, 1993.

——. *Assessment Standards for School Mathematics.* Reston, Va: National Council of Teachers of Mathematics, 1995.

——. *Curriculum and Evaluation Standards for School Mathematics.* Reston, Va: National Council of Teachers of Mathematics, 1989.

Norwood, Karen, and Glenda Carter. "Journal Writing: An Insight into Students' Understanding." *Teaching Children Mathematics* 1 (November 1994): 146–48.

Public Broadcasting Service. *PBS MATHLINE.* Alexandria, Va.: Public Broadcasting Service, 1994.

Sammons, Kay B., Beth Kobett, Joan Heiss, and Francis Fennell. "Linking Instruction and Assessment in the Mathematics Classroom." *Arithmetic Teacher* 39 (February 1992): 11–16.

Schoenfeld, Alan, Hugh Burkhardt, Phil Daro, Jim Ridgway, Judah Schwartz, and Sandra Wilcox. *Balanced Assessment for the Mathematics Curriculum.* Menlo Park, Calif.: Dale Seymour Publications, 1998.

Shaw, Jean M., Conn Thomas, Ann Hoffman, and Janis Bulgren. "Using Concept Diagrams to Promote Understanding in Geometry. *Teaching Children Mathematics* 2 (November 1995): 184–89.

Shuard, Hilary, and Andrew Rothery, eds. *Children Reading Mathematics.* London: Anthenaeum Press, 1984.

Spangler, Denise A. "Assessing Students' Beliefs." *Arithmetic Teacher* 40 (November 1992): 148–52.

Stenmark, Jean K. *Assessment Alternatives in Mathematics: An Overview of Assessment Techniques That Promote Learning.* Berkeley, Calif.: Lawrence Hall of Science, 1989.

——, ed. *Mathematics Assessment: Myths, Models, Good Questions, and Practical Suggestions.* Reston, Va: National Council of Teachers of Mathematics, 1991.

——, ed. *101 Short Problems for EQUALS.* Berkeley, Calif.: University of California, 1995.

Stenmark, Jean K., Pam Beck, and Harold Asturias. "A Room with More Than One View." *Mathematics Teaching in the Middle School* 1 (April 1994): 44–49.

Stiggins, Richard J. *Student-Centered Classroom Assessment.* New York: Macmillan College Publishing, 1994

Swan, Malcolm. "Assessing Mathematical Processes: The English Experience." *Mathematics Teaching in the Middle School* 1 (March-April 1996): 706–11.

Tonack, De A. "A Teacher's View on Classroom Assessment: What and How." *Mathematics Teaching in the Middle School* 2 (November-December 1996): 70–73.

WBGH Educational Foundation. *Assessment Library for Grades K–12.* Boston: WGBH Educational Foundation, 1998.

Warloe, Kris. "Assessment as a Dialogue: A Means of Interacting with Middle School Students." In *Assessment in the Mathematics Classroom.* 1993 Yearbook of the National Council of Teachers of Mathematics, edited by Norman Webb, pp. 152–58. Reston, Va: National Council of Teachers of Mathematics, 1993.

Wiggins, Grant. "Honesty and Fairness: Toward Better Grading and Reporting." In *Communicating Student Learning: 1996 ASCD Yearbook*, edited by Thomas Gershey, pp. 141–71. Alexandria, Va: Association for Supervision and Curriculum Development, 1996.

Zawojewski, Judith S. "Polishing a Data Task: Seeing Better Assessment. *Teaching Children Mathematics* 2 (February 1996): 372–78.

Zawojewski, Judith S., and Richard Lesh. "Scores and Grades: What are the Problems? What are the Alternatives? *Mathematics Teaching in the Middle School* 1 (May 1996): 776–79.

Index